Managing Traumatic Stress Through Art

Managing Traumatic Stress Through Art

Managing Traumatic Stress Through Art

DRAWING FROM THE CENTER

Barry M. Cohen, Mary-Michola Barnes, and Anita B. Rankin

The Sidran Press
2328 W. Joppa Rd.
Suite 15
Lutherville, MD 21093
(410) 825-8888

International Standard Book Number: 0-9629164-7-1.
Library of Congress Card Catalogue Number: 95-068155.
Printed in the United States of America.

Frame images from the Pictorial Archive Series are provided and copyrighted by Dover Publications, Inc.

Pattern and texture images are provided and copyrighted by Dover Publications, Inc. and F & W Publications, Inc.

Book and icon design by Barry M. Cohen, Mary-Michola Barnes, Anita Rankin, and Paul Hotvedt.

For Joan A. Turkus, M.D.,
with deepest respect

Contents

SECTION ONE   DEVELOPING BASIC TOOLS FOR MANAGING DISTRESS

SECTION TWO   ACKNOWLEDGING AND REGULATING YOUR EMOTIONS

SECTION THREE   BEING AND FUNCTIONING IN THE WORLD

Note to Our Readers

■ *What are the skills one needs to cope with unforeseen misfortune?*

■ *How can one find a way to express feelings that cannot be put into words?*

■ *Where does one find creative pathways toward hopefulness and well-being?*

This workbook, created for you and others who have experienced the inescapable aftereffects of trauma, can help you to discover some of the answers to these questions.

Self-healing and creativity are natural human processes that together can help you to cope, express feelings, and work toward well-being. In fact, throughout the ages people have used creative expression to travel inward to places where words are seldom found.

No two people have the same journey toward recovery. Whatever healing path you follow, we believe it will be illuminated by this workbook. Know that the images and words that emerge from these art experiences are your own and they can provide you with a creative direction to wellness.

Healing is not a solitary endeavor. Everyone, no matter how self-sufficient, needs someone to listen and care. For this reason, we recommend you find the appropriate people to encourage, support, and inspire you as you embark on your path to healing.

Be assured that so-called *artistic talent* is not necessary to benefit from this workbook. Only a willingness to try new ways of expressing yourself is required.

Foreword

It is so difficult to put the complexities of the trauma recovery process into words—artwork does it so much better! For this reason, among others, I readily agreed to write the foreword to this workbook, written by my colleagues at THE CENTER: Post-Traumatic & Dissociative Disorders Program, art therapists Barry M. Cohen, Mary-Michola Barnes, and Anita B. Rankin. As a physician and psychiatrist, I greatly value and consistently advocate for the importance of expressive therapies in the process of healing and recovery for those suffering from post-traumatic stress. Although I did expect to see my conceptual framework that focuses on pacing and containing reflected in the book, I did not anticipate the awe and delight that I experienced in my first reading of *Managing Traumatic Stress through Art.* I am deeply touched by the clarity and creativity of the authors. Through their theoretical and clinical expertise in art therapy, they have contributed something much needed by clients and therapists working with the aftereffects of traumatic stress. Cohen, Barnes, and Rankin have structured and presented art experiences in which both artwork and reflective writing are integral parts of a protected, healing journey through the pain of recovery into a new, creative phase of life.

This workbook addresses the stages of post-traumatic stress recovery with wisdom and simplicity. The first section is devoted to establishing a safe framework for trauma resolution. The second section deals with acknowledging and regulating emotion; it helps the trauma survivor make sense of confusing and overwhelming emotional experiences. Reflective writing segments allow for ongoing integration of thinking and feeling. The final section focuses on self and relational development and improved functioning and growth. The art experiences presented are broad enough to be relevant to those recovering from a wide variety of traumatic experiences ranging from childhood abuse to disabling medical illness. Directions for the art exercises are wonderfully clear. Carefully conceived written reflections at the end of each experience facilitate insight and balance. The entire workbook is infused with a sense of empowerment and hope.

Recovery is an active, creative, transformational process that plumbs the depth and breath of human potential. Words alone are not enough to make it happen. Recovery requires creative expression in symbol and metaphor, the type of expression in which these authors so carefully and gently guide the not-just reader, but do-er. It has been a privilege for me to see the art productions of over 1,000 trauma survivors who have come to THE CENTER for treatment. By choosing to welcome these art experiences into your life, you will open the door to your personal creativity and resilience.

Although "none of us is protected from trauma," as the authors state in the introduction, it is my belief that this workbook will help many victims of post-traumatic stress through the process of resolution and recovery. As more and more victims recover and all of us work together to grow into more conscious human beings, we can stop the preventable cycles of abuse and violence and provide hope for the children of future generations. I predict that this book will contribute significantly to that goal.

Joan Turkus, M.D.

How to Use this Workbook

To achieve a beneficial outcome from these art experiences, it is recommended that you
- read the introductory material provided at the beginning of each art experience,
- use only the art materials recommended,
- follow the artmaking steps carefully, and
- write your responses to the questions in the blank space provided in the workbook or in a separate notebook or journal.

The 26 art experiences are divided into three sections:
- I.   Developing Basic Tools for Managing Stress
- II. Acknowledging and Regulating Your Emotions
- III. Being and Functioning in the World

We recommend that you first complete the art experiences in Section I, because they can be used to manage distress, should it emerge while completing the remaining sections. If the art process, product, or writing ever becomes overwhelming to you, remove your work to a place where it cannot be seen and try one of the art experiences from Section I. You can continue to work on the unfinished project once you feel sufficiently stable.

The art experiences in Sections II and III may be completed in any order that you wish. You may find it beneficial to do some of the art experiences again and again; your pictorial imagery will undoubtedly change as your healing progresses.

Each art experience is divided into four parts:
- a brief overview of the subject to be addressed in the art experience, an estimate of the time you need to complete the experience, and a list of necessary art materials;
- a few questions to help you with GETTING STARTED on the artmaking process;
- step-by-step ARTMAKING GUIDELINES; and
- a chance to put some WRITTEN REFLECTIONS down on paper (or just think) about the art experience and consider ways to integrate these insights into your life.

Here are a few other tips to help you maximize your efforts:
- Gather all the art materials before starting the art activity, since disruptions are detrimental to the process.
- Provide yourself with adequate work space where you will not be interrupted by telephone calls, other people, or activities.
- Allow adequate time to finish the art experience in a single sitting.

It is not the purpose of this workbook to encourage you to produce gallery or professional quality art; please do not judge your creations according to those standards. These experiences are for the sole purpose of communicating with yourself (and possibly your therapist). There is no "right" or "wrong" result.

Preface

We three have shared the uncommon experience of working with hundreds of people whose lives have been disrupted by trauma. Again and again, we have seen trauma's debilitating effects eased by the benefits of creativity. However, when we were first presented with the opportunity to create an art-oriented workbook, our immediate response was one of trepidation. Because most people associate creative expression with the unbridled release of tension and feeling, we recognized the difficulty in designing safe, effective art experiences for use outside the therapy session. After months of provocative and thoughtful discussion, we identified a highly structured approach that would promote effective self-management of post-traumatic symptoms. Thus prepared, we embarked on this project ready to meet the creative challenges it posed.

Our core therapeutic philosophy is based on our years of working at THE CENTER, a program dedicated to progressive treatment of adults who experienced significant physical, sexual, and emotional abuse in childhood. The Empowerment Model of treatment developed by the directors of THE CENTER holds as its central tenet the client's need to function effectively in daily life while working toward lessening the aftereffects of traumatic stress. To that end, specialized education fostering self-reliance and mastery is of primary importance in the recovery process of each client. The art experiences in this workbook emerge directly from this approach; they encourage creative growth, each resulting in a validating, tangible extension of the self. The artwork and reflective writing focus on the acknowledgment of current life issues and the potential for personal transformation.

Now our excitement far exceeds our trepidation. It is our hope that this workbook will provide the reader with some of the knowledge, skills, and tools needed to move through traumatic experiences toward a life of increased comfort, balance, and well-being.

Acknowledgments

We gratefully acknowledge Esther Giller of the Sidran Foundation and Press for bringing this project to our attention. Her enthusiasm, support, and expertise allowed us to realize our goal in a relatively brief period of time. The patients and staff of THE CENTER: Post-Traumatic & Dissociative Disorders Program have provided us with an incomparable opportunity for learning and professional growth. Laura Howard, a trusted colleague and friend, consistently extended valuable suggestions and support. The approach we used to describe and select art materials is drawn from the work of Sandra Graves and Vija Lusebrink, pioneer theorists and clinicians in the field of art psychotherapy. Mary Isaacson, Mary Strigari, and the staff of the Sidran Press deftly edited our text during various phases of this endeavor. Similarly, members of the Kranafrantz family were always on hand with the right word or phrase when we found ourselves at a loss. Finally, we are indebted to art therapist and comrade, Anne Mills, for her much appreciated enthusiasm, gracious editing, and pragmatic contributions to our manuscript.

Introduction

None of us is protected from trauma, be it a one-time catastrophic event or a long-term hardship. From illness to violent crime, natural disasters to divorce, layoffs to accidents, abuse and domestic violence to war, such misfortunes can occur at any time in one's life. In addition to the traumas that happen directly to us and our bodies there are other kinds that invade our lives. They are no less disruptive, even though they are experienced secondhand. Witnessing trauma, be it by sight or sound, is another way that accidents, violence, illness, and disasters can affect us.

Many factors contribute to the impact of trauma: age, social and cultural influences, history of previous trauma, physical and psychological health, and quality of coping skills. However what is traumatic for one person may be only stressful for another. Support systems available at the time of the trauma and afterwards play a substantial role in how we cope. To deny pain in our lives is to walk a dangerous path that can lead to life-long dysfunction.

The aftereffects of trauma are both psychological and physiological. Feelings of helplessness and hopelessness contribute to changes in self-image and contaminate interpersonal relationships. Emotional flooding and numbing, chaotic and conflicted thought processes, and maladaptive behaviors are symptoms that can be related to being overwhelmed by trauma. Sleep disturbances, phobias, flashbacks, memory impairment, hypervigilance, physical pain, and addictions are other debilitating symptoms that can be related to post-traumatic stress.

No matter what the cause or origin of the trauma, adults are responsible for developing the necessary coping skills to move forward. With careful thought and daily practice, most people can recover a sense of safety and purpose in their lives; some will achieve even more effective and beneficial ways of functioning in the world than those they used before the trauma.

To overcome the impact of traumatic stress one needs to restore, or to develop, healthy ways to tolerate distress and pain, to have compassion and respect for oneself, to interact with others without compromising personal values and beliefs, and to make changes that allow for purpose and meaning in life. Creativity, a natural human function, plays an important role in the development of these abilities. This workbook offers an opportunity to everyone, regardless of previous experience or artistic talent, to manage symptoms of traumatic stress in a creative, life-affirming way.

Trauma and Treatment

Recovery from post-traumatic stress can be described as a three-part process: (1) physical and psychological stabilization, (2) discussion of the traumatic event, and (3) exploration and management of the aftereffects. This workbook uses art to externalize trauma's impact and to explore ways of managing its aftereffects; it is not an exhaustive guide to all the psychological tasks essential to complete understanding of the traumatic event and recovery from it. A trained specialist with whom you can review what happened and thoughtfully explore its meaning can be helpful. In fact, traumatized people who have had an opportunity to discuss their stories with trained, empathic professionals are typically more resilient to trauma's aftereffects.

If you find that artmaking with this workbook is helpful in your healing process, you may wish to include further art therapy in your recovery plan. The American Art Therapy Association (AATA, 1202 Allanson Road, Mundelein, IL 60060, 708-949-6064) will give you the name and phone number of a person from the AATA chapter in your area, who can provide you with a list of local registered art therapists.

It is also helpful to discuss your experiences and feelings with other trauma survivors to increase your understanding and acceptance of trauma's impact; this can instill hope. Joining a support group that focuses on the type of trauma you experienced can be beneficial to your recovery process. Consult your local community mental health agency for resources in your area.

Telling your traumatic story through talking, writing, or artwork can be retraumatizing if you have not yet attained an adequate level of emotional stability. Please refrain from using the art experiences in this workbook if you experience a dramatic increase in symptoms, such as debilitating anxiety or despair. Further, if your symptoms are severe or persistent, you are strongly advised to seek professional support and guidance from a trained, licensed professional.

Pacing and Containment

Traumatic experiences, whether a single event or a situation occurring over an extended period of time, are comprised of various elements: specific behaviors, emotions, physical sensations, and related thoughts. Unfortunately, people who have been subjected to extremely stressful situations have a tendency to recreate circumstances in their lives that are similar to those they have already endured. These re-enactments can be retraumatizing because they expose you again to elements of your original trauma, and retraumatization impedes progress toward health. Pacing and containment are two important techniques you can use to manage your healing process and avoid retraumatizing yourself.

Containment is the self-directed ability to control potentially retraumatizing material that arises in the form of unwanted or unresolved images, sensations, thoughts, and feelings. Use of containment as a tool allows you to store this overwhelming material for safe exploration at a later time and without causing distress to you in the present. Along with pacing, it is an essential component of the self-management of post-traumatic symptoms. Containment should not be confused with indefinitely avoiding certain emotions, thoughts, and sensations. It is a way to handle traumatic material in a decisive, empowered fashion. In other words, containment allows people to deal with traumatic material and responses in a safe, controlled manner.

Another important technique in the self-management of post-traumatic stress is pacing. Pacing allows you to control the speed and timing at which you work on your recovery issues in order to achieve the most positive results. It is key in monitoring where, when, and how healing work can be done. Pacing requires discipline and stamina. It is an important factor in transforming distress.

Psychological healing is a creative process. It requires time, the desire to achieve a new level of self-awareness, an active search for knowledge, and problem-solving skills. Metaphor is a vital component of creativity because it allows familiar circumstances to be seen in new ways; it enhances understanding and presents opportunities for change. Art uses visual thinking—the language of lines, shapes, forms, textures, and colors—to create metaphorical images that represent or symbolize ideas and objects. The creative art process uses visual metaphors and visual thinking to move through roadblocks, resolve crises, and transform internal conflict. Visual metaphors are images that stand for ideas, feelings, experiences, objects, sensations, or actions. For example, happiness could be represented by an upwardly moving squiggly line, a shining sun, or a happy face. A stomach ache could be shown by a tightly wound spiral, a carefully drawn knot of rope, or an abdomen with a big red spot in the middle.

Art externalizes experiences, hopes, and conflicts. Art can enable you to safely test a variety of options. Art does not have to be perfect. Art can help you to heal and to live. Thus, inner responses to trauma can be expressed in visual metaphors, which can then be modified or transformed. Changes in these visual metaphors can reflect changes in personal viewpoints or behavior. Transforming art images is unquestionably easier than transforming behavioral patterns, attitudes, or actual life situations, but the experience of making changes in your art can nonetheless help you begin to manage stress and make changes in your life.

Art Media and Artmaking

Just as people have distinct personality traits, so, too, do art materials. Media (as art materials are also called) can be placed along a continuum according to their inherent qualities, from *fluid* at one pole to *resistive* at the other. These media traits affect the artmaking process in different ways. It is therefore important to consider each medium's properties before selecting it for an art activity.

Fluid media (e.g., paints, oil pastels, chalk pastels, and clay) take less effort to manipulate, are sloppier, more difficult to control, and can have a loosening effect on your psychological defenses. If you attempt to express an overwhelming or intense emotion such as rage with fluid media like thick, sloppy paints, you might easily overstimulate yourself and lose control over the process and your defenses. On the other hand, if your feelings are not easily accessed, a fluid medium such as soft chalk pastel might facilitate sufficient loosening of your emotional armor, allowing feelings to surface.

Resistive media (e.g., lead and colored pencils, fine point markers, and magazine pictures) facilitate a greater release of energy, are neater, and allow for more technical precision in the hands of an untrained artist. Making collages from torn paper or devising problem-solving drawings are excellent ways to use resistive media. Such tasks allow you to remain in control and engage in conscious decision-making while using materials that are well-suited to the task. On the other hand, if control is your usual style, using a more fluid medium might be in order. An "in between" medium in this case would be oil pastels because they offer more fluidity of application, but are not as uncontrollable as watery paints. The greater your desire for release, the more beneficial resistive media can be. Just think about stone carvers pounding on a huge block of granite.

It bears repeating that understanding media traits is essential to the effective use of artmaking during trauma recovery. To ignore the interaction between maker and media is to chance retraumatization. Making conscious, informed media choices can empower and enhance your transformation of post-traumatic stress through creativity.

Essential Art Materials

The following is a list of basic materials that has been devised with cost in mind. You will be able to successfully complete all of the art experiences with either student or professional grade materials.

1. white drawing paper: 18" × 24" (can be purchased in sketchpads or in bulk)

2. construction paper: 18" × 24" (in assorted colors)

3. used magazines

4. lead pencil and eraser

5. oil pastels (also called craypas, box of 12 assorted colors)

6. colored pencils (box of 12 assorted colors)

7. acrylic paints (introductory student-quality set)

8. acrylic paintbrushes (1/2" round and 1" flat)

9. palette (a ceramic or plastic plate)

10. scissors

11. glue stick or rubber cement

Most of these materials can be found in art supply stores or ordered by mail from the companies listed on page 137.

The following art materials are used only in the art experience listed:

1. small sketch book, blank book, or loose-leaf notebook (Art Experiences 4 and 8)

2. box with a lid (for example, a shoe box, wooden box, tin box, oatmeal box) (Art Experience 6)

3. roll of waxed paper (Art Experiences 12 and 16)

4. electric iron (Art Experience 16)

5. two photocopies of a recent photograph of yourself (Art Experience 19)

6. assorted found papers (Art Experience 20)

SECTION ONE

Developing Basic Tools for Managing Distress

1 | Drawing a Breath

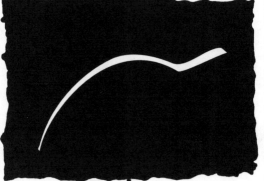

Post-traumatic stress can affect the way you breathe. Holding your breath, as well as breathing rapidly or shallowly may be related to chronic anxiety which can be a symptom of post-traumatic stress. Awareness and regulation of the quality of your breathing can have several positive effects. Slowing and deepening your breath allows for adequate intake of oxygen and output of carbon dioxide, both of which are necessary for physical well-being. Conscious breathing during times of distress can allow you to release muscular and emotional tension, reducing your level of distress. Focusing awareness on your breathing can shift your thoughts away from flashbacks and non-productive or obsessive thinking and bring your consciousness back into the present.

This art experience helps you to use the quality of your breathing to manage distress. You will be making two line drawings to depict the quality of your breathing.

Estimated Completion Time 45 - 60 minutes

Art Materials
- scratch paper
- one sheet of 18" × 24" white drawing paper cut into two 12" × 18" pieces
- black oil pastel

Getting Started

1. Sit in a comfortable chair and place your feet solidly on the floor. Notice the sensation of your feet pressing against the floor.

2. Notice the quality of your breathing by considering the following:
   - the depth of your breathing: shallow, deep, moderate
   - the rate of your breathing: fast, slow, moderate
   - the pause between the inhalation and exhalation of your breath
   - the expansion and contraction of your rib and abdominal areas
   - changes in the overall pattern of your breathing

Artmaking Guidelines

1. Practice drawing different kinds of lines with the oil pastel on scrap paper: long and short; thick and thin; curved and angular; quick and slow; light and heavy pressure; dashes and dots.

2. Focus on your breathing. As you are inhaling and exhaling, visualize your breath as a line and draw each breath with the oil pastel on the sheet of 12" × 18" white drawing paper. Use one or more types of lines to represent your breathing. Take about five minutes to record your breathing. If you feel comfortable doing so, close your eyes while you draw.

3. Alter the quality of your breathing until you achieve a more relaxed state by letting your abdomen expand when you are inhaling and contract when you are exhaling. As you are inhaling and exhaling, try saying silently to yourself: "breathing in calm, breathing out tension." You may want to substitute your own words for "calm" and "tension."

4. Draw your altered breathing on another sheet of 12" × 18" white drawing paper. Take about five minutes to record your breathing. Use one or more types of lines to depict each breath. Close your eyes while you are drawing, if you are comfortable doing so.

Drawing a Breath

MANAGING TRAUMATIC STRESS
THROUGH ART
© SIDRAN PRESS, 1995

Written Reflections

1. Describe the visual qualities of the lines in each of your drawings. (See DESCRIBING YOUR ART on page 135 for suggestions.)

2. Describe the similarities and differences between the two drawings. Compare both the quality/quantity of the lines and the use of space on the paper.

3. Consider how the line quality reflects your distress level.

4. Describe how you were able to consciously change the quality of your breathing and note the difference it made in your distress level.

5. You can use breath awareness as an indicator of your distress level. How would a drawing of your breathing differ if you were petting a dog, watching a scary movie, riding a ferris wheel, or watching the clouds go by on a lazy summer afternoon?

6. You can consciously change the quality of your breathing to reduce your stress level. Think of ways you can remind yourself to modify your breathing when you are experiencing distress. With practice, breath regulation will become more automatic.

Drawing a Breath

MANAGING TRAUMATIC STRESS
THROUGH ART
© SIDRAN PRESS, 1995

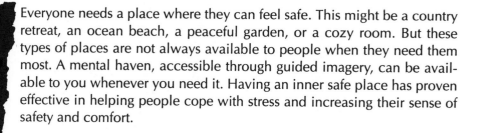

2 | Establishing a Safe Place

Everyone needs a place where they can feel safe. This might be a country retreat, an ocean beach, a peaceful garden, or a cozy room. But these types of places are not always available to people when they need them most. A mental haven, accessible through guided imagery, can be available to you whenever you need it. Having an inner safe place has proven effective in helping people cope with stress and increasing their sense of safety and comfort.

The use of an imaginary safe place is especially helpful for people who have experienced trauma. When fear, panic, or self-destructive thoughts become overwhelming, you can use your imagination to go to a restful inner sanctuary—a personal haven from the aftereffects of trauma and other life stresses—to regain a sense of safety, to restore strength, and to achieve a renewal of spirit.

This art experience helps you to create a drawing of an imaginary safe place that you can use as a tool to manage overwhelming stress.

Estimated Completion Time 45 - 60 minutes

Art Materials
■ one sheet of 18" × 24" white drawing paper
■ oil pastels, colored pencils, or acrylic paints (brushes, palette, and water)

Getting Started

1. List all the places, both real and imaginary, that have felt relatively secure and safe to you during the course of your life. (If you have never had an experience of a safe place, don't be discouraged. Try to imagine what such a place would be like.)

2. Take your time and allow yourself to begin to see, in your imagination, a place that feels safe to you. It can be real or imaginary, or have elements of both. You are in control of this visualization: If anything appears that makes you uneasy, you can replace it with something comforting. This safe place can be located anywhere: in a room, house, building, boat, or outdoor setting. This environment may be based on one or more of the safe places you listed above or you may want to create an entirely new safe place. Write some preliminary notes describing a safe place suitable for you.

3. List the features that you want to include in your safe place. These might be elements that are comfortable (pillows, blankets, furniture), familiar (meaningful items from among your possessions), or pleasurable (flowers, music, books).

Artmaking Guidelines

1. Draw your safe place using the art materials you have chosen. There are many ways to represent your safe place, from different points of view including aerial or side views, to a simple diagram or a more elaborate illustration.

2. Make a "security check" of your safe place and add any features that will enhance your sense of safety and comfort. For example, if your safe place is a room, you may want to add a door that can be closed or a window with a beautiful view.

Establishing a Safe Place

MANAGING TRAUMATIC STRESS THROUGH ART
© SIDRAN PRESS, 1995

Written Reflections

1. Imagine standing in your safe place. What do you see to the left and right of you, behind and in front of you, above and below you? (You may want to make a series of sketches representing each of these different viewpoints.)

2. List each of the visual features in your safe place picture.

3. Describe the significance and purpose of each feature.

**Establishing
a Safe Place**

MANAGING TRAUMATIC STRESS
THROUGH ART
© SIDRAN PRESS, 1995

8

4. Place your picture a few feet away and imagine it on a large screen. First, observe the picture in its entirety; next, carefully study its details. List the circumstances in which it might be helpful to use your imaginary safe place. For example, you can visualize your safe place for brief moments when you are in public and for longer periods of time when you are by yourself.

5. Create a step-by-step plan that will enable you to mentally get to your imaginary safe place. This plan might begin with a phrase such as "going to my safe place" or it might begin with the image of a flight of stairs that can take you to your safe place.

Note Practice visualizing the image so that you can see all details clearly even when your eyes are closed. Find a place where you can hang your safe place artwork and look at it regularly until you can consciously use it in your daily life. You may want to create an actual safe place in your living space. This could be a room or area of a room that is filled with objects that are comforting to you and help you to gain a sense of safety.

Establishing
a Safe Place

MANAGING TRAUMATIC STRESS
THROUGH ART
© SIDRAN PRESS, 1995

3 | *Protective Container*

People who have experienced personal trauma can often become overwhelmed by feelings or thoughts that can lead to non-productive and harmful behavior. If this has been an issue for you, learning to develop and to use containment images and techniques can improve your level of functioning and sense of well-being. Containment is a self-management tool that allows you to store overwhelming information, images, or feelings for exploration at a later time, without causing distress to you in the present. The concept of containment is different from advice such as "Pull yourself together and get on with your life" or "Just put the trauma behind you and don't think about it anymore."

Creating an image of a container to hold recurrent, intrusive material provides you with a method of self-control that can protect you from retraumatization. When you gain more control and become more emotionally stable, you can decide to examine some of these overwhelming thoughts, memories, feelings, or impulses. Then you can remove them, one at a time, from the container or containers you have created for their safe protection.

This art experience helps you create an image of a container to temporarily store intrusive thoughts and overwhelming feelings.

Estimated Completion Time 45 - 60 minutes

Art Materials
- one sheet of 18" × 24" white drawing paper
- colored pencils, oil pastels, or acrylic paints (brushes, palette, and water)

1. Identify one intrusive thought, overwhelming feeling, or unhealthy impulse that you would like to temporarily contain.

2. Spend a few minutes considering the necessary features of a container designed to safely hold this thought, feeling, or impulsive behavior. Think about its form, location, and function. The more personalized your image, the more effective this technique will be. You may design a simple or elaborate container. The following describes some containers and their characteristics:

- a chained trunk located under the sea, to confine traumatic flashbacks
- a locked room located at the end of a long corridor, for storage of overwhelming feelings
- a video cassette located on a shelf in a remote study, to provide for later viewing of traumatic events
- a filing cabinet located in a vault, for organizing information related to the trauma
- a protective bubble located on a cloud, to hold unpleasant body sensations

Your container should have some way to be securely closed, and a way to be reopened, over which you have complete control.

Protective Container

MANAGING TRAUMATIC STRESS
THROUGH ART
© SIDRAN PRESS, 1995

Artmaking Guidelines

1. Draw a picture of your container.

2. Consider the location that would best suit your container. Add these surroundings to your picture.

3. Study your drawing. Add any features necessary to make your container more effective.

Written Reflections

1. Describe your container in writing. Be as specific as possible about its physical characteristics and location.

2. Explain why the various features of your container are significant to you.

MANAGING TRAUMATIC STRESS
THROUGH ART
© SIDRAN PRESS, 1995

3. Outline the steps you must take to place overwhelming material into your container. For instance, you could close your eyes and imagine the following:

- a symbolic object to represent the unsafe feeling, thought, or sensation
- wrapping this object up; perhaps labelling it
- placing this package in the container
- closing the container securely

Note Practice these steps to build your confidence in using this technique. You can visualize your container when you are alone or in public to temporarily contain overwhelming feelings and thoughts. You may find that you require different types of containers for various feelings, memories, or sensations. This art experience can be used again each time you wish to modify a container or create a new one.

Protective
Container

MANAGING TRAUMATIC STRESS
THROUGH ART
© SIDRAN PRESS, 1995

4 Sensory Relief

One type of response to traumatic experiences is avoidance of sensory stimuli (scents, tastes, sights, sounds, textures) associated with the trauma. This reaction might unfortunately result in the deprivation of pleasant and soothing sensory stimuli that might otherwise decrease anxiety or fear. Actively choosing to give yourself positive sensory experiences can be empowering. Visiting a greenhouse or garden to smell herbs and flowers, going to a fabric store to touch soft and luxurious textures, enjoying the taste of a ripe peach or pear, and listening to soft music are some examples of self-soothing activities that are directly linked to the senses.

It is not always possible to soothe yourself through actual life experiences; sometimes it is more convenient to use your imagination. You can use pictures to invoke imaginary sensations that help you shift from a state of distress to one of relative calm. In this way, you can provide yourself with a relaxing break during stressful or unpleasant periods.

In this art experience, you will compile a "relief book" of images to reduce distress by helping you to conjure up positive sensory experiences.

Estimated Completion Time 60 - 90 minutes

Art Materials
- choice of a small sketch book, blank book, or loose-leaf notebook with unlined paper
- magazines
- scissors
- glue

Getting Started

List sensory experiences in each of the following categories that are pleasant for you:

■ SCENTS

■ SOUNDS

■ TASTES

■ TEXTURES

■ SIGHTS

Artmaking Guidelines

1. Look through magazines for pictures of things that are pleasant or soothing examples of each sensory category. Select and cut out as many examples of each category as you wish.

2. Glue each picture onto a separate page of your book.

3. Decorate or personalize your book cover, if you wish.

Sensory
Relief

MANAGING TRAUMATIC STRESS
THROUGH ART
© SIDRAN PRESS, 1995

Written Reflections

1. Describe the sensations, thoughts, and feelings you experienced while selecting the pictures for your book.

2. Notice which sensory categories you favored over the others. Often, people are more attuned to certain types of sensory input than to others. You may want to find ways to increase your awareness of and exposure to pleasant sensory experiences in categories that you least favor. List a few ideas here.

3. Include notes in your book to describe the significant elements each picture offers. You can write on the back of each page, if you wish.

4. Use your relief book to take a break from your routine or to lower your level of stress. List some circumstances when you might benefit from using your relief book.

5. Look through the pictures in your book and choose one that is particularly soothing or pleasant. Take a minute or so to focus on the picture, allowing yourself to enter into the sensory realm of the picture. Closing your eyes briefly might help you to enhance the effect.

Sensory
Relief

MANAGING TRAUMATIC STRESS
THROUGH ART
© SIDRAN PRESS, 1995

5 | Support Net

We get by—even during the best of times—with a little help from our friends. When you are coping with the impact of a trauma, supportive people can become even more important to you. Support systems are made up of individuals and groups that help you to continue on in the face of adversity; they provide the hope, spirit, and encouragement that you need to participate fully in your day-to-day life and personal development.

It is important to take the time to evaluate your support system in the wake of any trauma. Traumatic experiences can contribute to your alienation from those who might otherwise help you. You might also find that your support system is no longer adequate to meet your present needs. You may, however, discover (or rediscover) support resources that you did not realize were available to you, or that you were not using.

This art experience helps you to create a woven paper net symbolizing the various members and components of your support system.

Estimated Completion Time 45 - 60 minutes

Essential Art Materials

- one sheet of 18" × 24" white drawing paper cut up into four 9" × 12" pieces
- one sheet of 18" × 24" white drawing paper cut up into two 12" × 18" pieces
- colored pencils, oil pastels, or acrylic paints (brushes, palette, and water)
- scissors
- glue

1. Identify the components and members of your support system. Here are some suggestions:

- individuals: friends, family, teachers, mentors, therapists, spiritual/religious advisors, other admired individuals, pets

- groups: social, therapy, hobby, discussion

2. List 6 -10 of your supports below in a column on the left side.

3. Imagine a symbolic strand of material to represent each component or member of your support system. Here are some suggestions:

- type: filament, thread, string, twine, yarn, rope, or chain
- material: wool, cotton, silk, nylon, sisal, metal, plastic, synthetic, beads
- color and thickness of the strand
- other details: straight, curly, pliable, brittle, fuzzy, sharp, rough, soft

Write a description of the strand you chose to symbolically represent each component and member of your support system in the space next to their name above.

Support Net

MANAGING TRAUMATIC STRESS
THROUGH ART
© SIDRAN PRESS, 1995

Artmaking Guidelines

1. Draw the image of each symbolic strand side-by-side lengthwise on a sheet or two of 9" × 12" white drawing paper, leaving some space between each. You may want to label each of the strands with the name of the corresponding support.

2. Cut each strand into a separate strip.

3. Separate the strips into two equal piles.

4. Line up the strips from one pile vertically across the central section of a sheet of 18" × 24" white drawing paper, leaving at least 1/2" between each strip.

5. Glue the top 1/2" of each strip onto the sheet of paper. Allow the glue to dry.

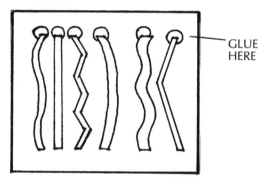

GLUE HERE

6. Weave the second set of strips horizontally across the first set, bringing the leading end of each strip behind the first vertical, in front of the next, behind the third, and so on. This will create a "basket weave" effect.

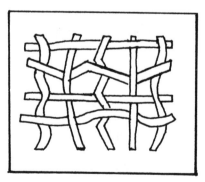

Support Net

7. Glue the ends of all strips to the sheet of paper.

MANAGING TRAUMATIC STRESS
THROUGH ART
© SIDRAN PRESS, 1995

Written Reflections

1. Look at the support net you have created. What are your first impressions? Does your support net look strong, weak, sufficient, small, or large?

2. Explain why you chose to represent each support source using the particular type of strand you chose. In your explanation of the strands include factors such as versatility, flexibility, size, strength, and durability.

3. Identify several types of situations when you typically need external support.

   ■ Do you recognize the need for support at the time?
   ■ Do you ask for support?
   ■ If not, why?

4. Explain how each of your current sources of support are helpful to you.

5. Explore ideas for improving your existing support system. List other types of people, services, or groups that could strengthen your system.

6. List any changes you would like to make in your support system at this time. Develop a plan to accomplish these changes.

Support Net

MANAGING TRAUMATIC STRESS
THROUGH ART
© SIDRAN PRESS, 1995

6 | *Comfort Box*

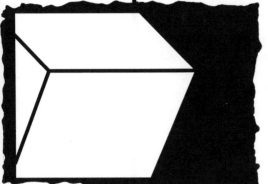

When people who have been traumatized become overwhelmed with feelings such as anxiety, anger, fear, or despair, they are often unable to soothe or stabilize themselves. The intensity of these overwhelming feelings can leave you feeling helpless and unable to draw on inner strengths or external supports. At these times it is helpful to have a tangible source of comfort that is easily available and personally meaningful.

This art experience allows you to create a box to use when you are overwhelmed or in distress that will hold personal resources for hope and comfort.

Estimated Completion Time 60 - 90 minutes

Art Materials

- a box with a lid (for example, a shoe box, wooden box, tin box, oatmeal box) or cardboard to construct one
- materials for decoration (such as acrylic paints, construction paper, fabric, tissue paper, magazine pictures)
- scissors
- glue

1. List some things that have provided you with comfort in the past, such as events, images, pieces of writing, or objects.

2. Note colors and textures that are comforting to you.

3. List comforting items, such as pictures, poems, and photos that you could put into your box.

Comfort
Box

MANAGING TRAUMATIC STRESS
THROUGH ART
© SIDRAN PRESS, 1995

23

Artmaking Guidelines

1. Choose or construct a box that will meet your requirements to hold personal items. Consider size, shape, and durability.

2. Focus on the exterior of your box and imagine what type of decoration would give it comforting qualities. Consider glued or painted decoration, colors, images, fabrics, and textures.

3. Decorate the outside of your box and lid, taking as much time as you wish; this part of the project can be soothing in itself.

4. Contemplate the interior of your box, keeping in mind that it will hold soothing and personally significant items. Decorate it accordingly.

5. Find at least one photo, poem, letter, sketch, magazine clipping, or object that suggests comfort to you and place it inside your new box.

Written Reflections

1. Describe how you decorated your comfort box, and in what way it is significant for you.

2. List the items and images you have placed into your comfort box thus far and write about their significance.

MANAGING TRAUMATIC STRESS
THROUGH ART
© SIDRAN PRESS, 1995

24

3. List other types of things you might place in your box.

4. Explore ideas about when and how you might use your comfort box in the future.

Note You can use your comfort box as a source of solace in times of need. You may want to include a few written statements such as: "I've made it through times like this before, I can do it again"; "I think I can learn to do it"; "Feelings change—this will pass"; "I am doing the best I am capable of doing right now." Continue to add to your comfort box's contents. Remember to place your box somewhere private, but accessible; you will want to find it easily when you need comfort.

Comfort
Box

MANAGING TRAUMATIC STRESS
THROUGH ART
© SIDRAN PRESS, 1995

7 | *Paving the Way*

Following trauma, people tend to feel more vulnerable, fragile, and in greater need of help from others. Yet, in dealing with the aftermath of trauma, your inner strengths are an essential resource in the development or restoration of your well-being.

It is helpful to realize that trauma can affect a person's strengths in various ways; certain strengths may become compromised, others may become more pronounced, and new strengths may even be developed. For instance, a person who used a sense of humor to deal with problematic events prior to a serious trauma may no longer find this strategy effective. The same person may, however, find that using organizational skills more assertively aids in preventing or reducing daily stress. In this case, one strength was compromised (sense of humor) while another strength was enhanced (organization).

Some inner strengths commonly beneficial in the effective management of traumatic stress are:

- **DETERMINATION** to overcome the trauma
- **WILL** to struggle and succeed
- **FAITH** in yourself and supportive people
- **COURAGE** to explore the circumstances and aftereffects of trauma
- **RESPONSIBILITY** to meet one's own needs
- **CREATIVITY** to imagine inner balance
- **RESILIENCE** to stress
- **OPEN-MINDEDNESS** for growth

This art experience provides guidelines for constructing a metaphoric path leading from traumatic stress to well-being. You will be identifying personal strengths to help you along that path; they are your stepping stones.

Estimated Completion Time 60 – 90 minutes

Art Materials

- one 18" × 24" sheet of white drawing paper
- assorted colors of construction paper
- scissors
- glue
- pencil

1. List 5 – 10 strengths that you possess. (See DESCRIBING YOUR STRENGTHS on page 134.)

2. Describe how your inner strengths have been affected by the trauma.

3. Identify any new strengths that you have developed as a result of the trauma.

Paving the
Way

MANAGING TRAUMATIC STRESS
THROUGH ART
© SIDRAN PRESS, 1995

27

Artmaking Guidelines

1. Choose a piece of colored paper to represent each strength you listed in GETTING STARTED #1 and #3.

2. Cut out several stepping stone shapes (about 1" in diameter) from each piece of paper. Label every colored shape with the name of the strength it represents.

3. Choose a piece of colored paper to represent each of the strengths listed below:

   - **DETERMINATION** to overcome the trauma
   - **WILL** to struggle and succeed
   - **FAITH** in myself and supportive others
   - **COURAGE** to explore circumstances and aftereffects of my trauma
   - **RESPONSIBILITY** to meet my personal needs
   - **CREATIVITY** to imagine inner balance
   - **RESILIENCE** to stress
   - **OPEN-MINDEDNESS** for growth

4. Cut out another set of stepping stone shapes and label each shape with one of the corresponding strengths listed above in ARTMAKING GUIDELINE #3.

5. Design a path representing your recovery process. This could be a winding, straight, spiral, or maze-like path. It may begin or end in the middle or toward the edge of the paper. Draw the outline of your path onto the paper, making the path wide enough to accommodate the stepping stones.

6. Cut a shape from a piece of colored paper (approximately 2" in diameter) to represent your trauma. Glue this where your path begins.

7. Choose another color of paper and cut a shape (approximately 2" in diameter) to represent a state of well-being. Glue this to the end point of your path.

8. Place all the stepping stones you created in ARTMAKING GUIDELINES #2 and #3 along the path, starting at the trauma shape and ending at the well-being shape.

9. Glue the stepping stone shapes to the paper when you have arrived at a satisfactory arrangement.

Paving the
Way

MANAGING TRAUMATIC STRESS
THROUGH ART
© SIDRAN PRESS, 1995

Written Reflections

1. Describe why you chose particular colors to represent particular strengths.

2. Consider the design of your path. How does it represent your expectations and attitude about the recovery process?

3. Think about where you are on the path at the present moment.

4. Describe new strengths that you would like to add to your path.

5. Identify a few ways to develop one of the strengths listed above in WRITTEN REFLECTION #4.

Note You can refer to your artwork when you are stuck on your recovery path. It can help you to identify which strength you need to tap, stabilize, or further develop to continue moving forward.

Paving the Way

MANAGING TRAUMATIC STRESS
THROUGH ART
© SIDRAN PRESS, 1995

8 | *Getaway Guidebook*

Dissociation or "spacing out" is a mental process used by many traumatized people to disconnect from stressful experiences. When physical escape is impossible, mental escape from intolerable or harmful situations may be the only way to survive severe trauma while it is occurring. However, using dissociation as an ordinary coping technique on a continual basis interferes with effective functioning. For instance, it can compromise your safety if you are not aware of what is going on in your surroundings at all times. Constant dissociation prevents you from experiencing your life as you live it, because you are not able to stay in the present. Getting away from distress is necessary on occasion, but is best accomplished with full awareness and self-control; you should retain a measure of connection to your present surroundings and be able to fully return to reality the moment you choose to do so.

This art experience helps you to design and use a picture guidebook for imaginary mini-vacations from stress.

Estimated Completion Time 45 - 60 minutes

Art Materials

- choice of a sketch book, blank book, or loose-leaf notebook
- magazines
- scissors
- glue

Getting Started

List some places where you have felt relaxed. This may include places where you have vacationed as well as places in your immediate locale that you find pleasant.

Artmaking Guidelines

1. Examine a variety of magazines and select the following types of pictures from them:

   ■ pleasant or comfortable places to be — outdoors
   ■ pleasant or comfortable places to be — indoors

2. Cut the pictures out.

3. Arrange and glue each of your pictures on a separate page of your book so that you will be able to view only one picture at a time.

4. Decorate, personalize, and title your book cover, if you wish.

Getaway Guidebook

MANAGING TRAUMATIC STRESS
THROUGH ART
© SIDRAN PRESS, 1995

Written Reflections

1. Study the images you selected for your guidebook and consider their appealing qualities.

2. Imagine you are actually in one of the pictures you have chosen for your guidebook and answer the following questions:

- Are you standing, sitting, or moving?

- Where, exactly, in this environment are you located?

- What is the temperature?

- What is the time of day?

- Describe the sights, sounds, and smells.

- What are you wearing?

- Do you prefer to be alone in this place?

- Who would you like to join you in this place?

- How do the objects in this place add to your sense of relaxation or enjoyment?

Getaway
Guidebook

MANAGING TRAUMATIC STRESS
THROUGH ART
© SIDRAN PRESS, 1995

3. Write a plan for using your Getaway Guidebook. Consider when you might want or need to use your guidebook in your current day-to-day life. You can use your Getaway Guidebook to take a 1 - 10 minute mini-vacation when you are feeling stressed.

Note You may want to write the questions (listed in WRITTEN REFLECTION #2) in your guidebook for easy reference to help you more readily enter into the pictured place each time you use your guidebook. You may wish to make a pocket-size version of this project to have with you when you are away from home.

Getaway
Guidebook

MANAGING TRAUMATIC STRESS
THROUGH ART
© SIDRAN PRESS, 1995

Anatomy of Self-Care

Attention to the basics of eating, resting, and physical activity is especially important following a traumatic experience. It is difficult or impossible for most people to handle the emotional aspects of recovery work if physical well-being is neglected. Establishing a sense of safety and control includes getting timely medical checkups and treatment, adequate nutrition, appropriate physical exercise, sufficient sleep, and rest. It is also important to engage in activities that provide a sense of comfort, leisure, and well-being. Activities of this sort may include a relaxing bath or shower, listening to soothing music, meditating, massaging your hands or feet, enjoying a cup of tea, treating yourself to a special event, playing with pets, or reading a book.

This art experience will help you to explore self-care issues and generate your own ideas for developing and using self-nurturing activities by creating a magazine picture collage.

Estimated Completion Time 60 - 90 minutes

Art Materials
- one sheet of 18" × 24" white drawing paper
- magazine pictures
- scissors
- glue

MANAGING TRAUMATIC STRESS
THROUGH ART
© SIDRAN PRESS, 1995

Getting Started

1. Describe how your ability to take care of yourself has changed since the trauma.

2. List some of your new self-care needs that have arisen as a result of the trauma.

3. List ways you are currently caring for yourself.

4. Note any areas of self-care that you would like to develop.

Artmaking Guidelines

1. Select and cut out several magazine pictures to represent current and desired aspects of your emotional, mental, and physical well-being. Any kind of image may be used to depict body/mind health, including landscapes, objects, foods, tools, machines, textures, or colors. Do not limit your selections to pictures of body parts, although you may wish to incorporate a few pictures of body parts in your collage.

2. Arrange these pictures so that the overall composition suggests the shape of a human body. Decide which images best function in your composition as a head, neck, chest, abdomen, arm, leg, hand, and foot. Move the pictures around on the 18" × 24" sheet of white drawing paper until you are satisfied with the composition.

3. Glue the pictures to the paper.

Anatomy of
Self-Care

MANAGING TRAUMATIC STRESS
THROUGH ART
© SIDRAN PRESS, 1995

Written Reflections

1. Consider the symbolic significance of each magazine picture in relation to the body part it represents.

2. Explain the relationship between each of the magazine pictures and your self-care needs.

3. Note any significance in the overall position or form of the figure you created.

MANAGING TRAUMATIC STRESS
THROUGH ART
© SIDRAN PRESS, 1995

36

4. Develop a realistic plan to improve the following basic categories of self-care:

   diet / nutrition

   sleep / rest

   exercise / activity

5. Make a list of activities that promote comfort, leisure, and overall well-being and explain how they relate to each of the pictures. Your list might include activities such as tending your garden, wearing comfortable slippers at home, talking a walk in the woods, buying yourself a flower, browsing in a bookstore, or going to a museum.

SECTION TWO

Acknowledging and Regulating Your Emotions

10 Landscapes of Emotion

Most people, at one time or another, must struggle to identify their feelings. The traumatized person, in particular, may have difficulty identifying and clarifying feelings. Further, the inability to access feelings may have been developed during the traumatic event, when emotions were unbearable. The ability to suppress or "shut away" emotions at that time was an indispensable part of coping and may even have been necessary for survival. Following trauma, the perceived need to continue suppressing negative emotions may lead to different degrees of "cutting off" both unpleasant and pleasant feelings. The state in which a person is no longer feeling any emotions is called *emotional numbing.*

Reconnecting with feelings is important, because feelings direct our attention and signal the need for change, protection, or care. Feelings also allow us to experience our lives with a sense of satisfaction and to establish relationships with others. In addition to recognizing that all feelings are significant, it is important to realize that all feelings change with time. Anger may give way to rage or courage. Fear may evolve into paranoia or sensible cautiousness. Sadness may lead to despair or empathy. An unexpected moment of joy may lift feelings of depression. Realizing that emotions change allows you to enjoy the times when you are happy, as well as to endure the times when you are in emotional pain. The ability to respond to all emotions with grace and compassion is a lifelong challenge.

You will be creating two landscape drawings in this art experience. In Part 1, you will safely identify current feelings. Part 2 encourages you to formulate a metaphorical change in your feeling state.

Estimated Completion Time 60 - 90 minutes

Art Materials
- one sheet of 18" × 24" white drawing paper cut into two 12" × 18" pieces
- colored pencils, oil pastels, or acrylic paints (brush, palette, and water)

MANAGING TRAUMATIC STRESS
THROUGH ART
© SIDRAN PRESS, 1995

Getting Started

1. Imagine what type of outdoor landscape might represent your current emotional state. Consider various landscape elements such as mountains, hills, valleys, plains, deserts, oceans, lakes, rivers, streams, waterfalls, trees, bushes, plants, flowers, boulders, rocks, and pebbles to mentally construct the appropriate landscape.

2. Imagine the climate or weather conditions in your landscape. Your choice should also relate to your current emotional state. Options include cold, cool, warm, hot, stormy, sunny, cloudy, partly overcast, rainy, snowy, windy, dry, and humid.

Artmaking Guidelines

Draw your imagined landscape using your choice of drawing materials on a sheet of 12" × 18" paper. Allow your picture to evolve as you draw and add details.

Landscapes of Emotion

MANAGING TRAUMATIC STRESS
THROUGH ART
© SIDRAN PRESS, 1995

41

Written Reflections

1. Describe how a person would feel if he or she were standing in different areas of this landscape. Refer to emotional feelings as well as physical sensations in your written description.

2. Imagine what this person would like to do in the different areas of this landscape. For instance, would this person want to seek shelter, sit down and relax, go for a swim, or run away?

3. List all the features in your landscape and match each to one or more feelings. (See DESCRIBING YOUR FEELINGS on page 132.) For instance, a solitary bush could represent the feeling of loneliness.

Getting Started

Imagine changing the landscape you completed in Part 1, through any or all of the following:

- addition or substitution of a different landscape feature

- rearrangement of the landscape

- reduction or enlargement of a specific feature in the landscape

- change in the weather and/or climatic conditions

Artmaking Guidelines

Create another landscape drawing. Incorporate the changes you imagined above in GETTING STARTED. Allow your landscape to evolve as you are drawing, adding or changing details through color, texture, or any other transformations of the image.

Landscapes of Emotion

MANAGING TRAUMATIC STRESS
THROUGH ART
© SIDRAN PRESS, 1995

43

Written Reflections

1. Describe how a person would feel if he or she were standing in different areas of the landscape. Include a description of this person's emotional feelings and physical sensations.

2. Imagine what this person would like to do in different areas of the landscape. For instance, would this person like to dance, walk, rest, look up at the stars, roll in the grass, fall down, run?

3. List each element in the landscape and match it with a feeling word. (See DESCRIBING YOUR FEELINGS on page 132.)

4. Place the two landscape drawings side-by-side and note their similarities and differences.

5. Consider why you might prefer being in one landscape more than the other.

Note You may wish to explore various options by creating several landscapes showing different transformations. Compare them with each other and choose the one that seems to represent the best alternative for you at this time.

Landscapes
of Emotion

MANAGING TRAUMATIC STRESS
THROUGH ART
© SIDRAN PRESS, 1995

11 | *Modifying Emotional Patterns*

Emotions are a combination of responses that people have to themselves and their environments. Any given emotional state typically includes several different feelings, even though you seem to experience only one emotion at a time. Emotions are interconnected with thoughts and behaviors, each influencing the others directly or indirectly. Because of this, it is possible to influence your feelings by making behavioral choices. This does not necessarily mean that you can change your emotional state at will (some intense emotional states will only fade with time), but since behavior is more easily controlled than emotions, engaging in certain behaviors can be helpful in regulating your emotional state. By choosing to influence your emotions, you can regain or develop a sense of control and improve your daily functioning.

This art experience is designed to help you identify feelings, recognize the need to modify feelings, and devise an action plan to influence your feelings through behavior. You will be creating a mixed media collage.

Estimated Completion Time 45 - 60 minutes

Art Materials
- one sheet of 18" × 24" white drawing paper
- graphic patterns in the APPENDIX
- colored pencils
- scissors
- glue

1. Make a list of several things you can do to soothe intense feelings. You may want to include activities such as going for a swim, taking a leisurely walk, reading an inspirational poem, listening to soft music, or calling a friend.

2. Make a list of several things you can do to invigorate or energize feelings of numbness, tiredness, or boredom. You might include activities such as taking a brisk walk, listening to lively music, eating a nutritious snack, reading an intellectually stimulating article, or taking a short nap if you have not slept adequately the night before.

Modifying
Emotional
Patterns

MANAGING TRAUMATIC STRESS
THROUGH ART
© SIDRAN PRESS, 1995

Artmaking Guidelines

1. Look through the graphic patterns in the APPENDIX. Select several patterns to represent various feelings that you are experiencing at this time, that you have recently experienced, or that are familiar to you.

2. Cut or tear the graphic patterns into shapes that further symbolize the feelings.

3. Place the shapes on a sheet of 18" × 24" white drawing paper. Move the shapes around the surface of the page until you find an arrangement that conveys meaning for you.

4. Glue the shapes to the white paper.

5. Look at the picture you have just created. Notice if there are areas that might symbolically benefit from enhanced energy. If so, choose a colored pencil that represents energy to you and apply it where needed.

6. Notice if any areas need to be soothed. Choose a colored pencil that represents a sense of calmness for you. Apply this color to those specific areas of the drawing.

Written Reflections

1. Look at your collage from a distance. How would you describe the overall "feeling" of the artwork?

2. Select words from DESCRIBING YOUR FEELINGS (page 132), matching one or more words to each of the graphic patterns you selected.

MANAGING TRAUMATIC STRESS
THROUGH ART
© SIDRAN PRESS, 1995

48

3. Describe the ways in which you used the colors to modify the feeling patterns.

4. Consider activities that might soothe or energize your feelings now. Consult the lists you made in GETTING STARTED for possibilities.

5. Choose one of the possible activities you listed above in WRITTEN REFLECTION #4 and take the time to follow through with that activity.

Modifying
Emotional
Patterns

MANAGING TRAUMATIC STRESS
THROUGH ART
© SIDRAN PRESS, 1995

12 | Layered Feelings

People normally experience a wide range of feelings—both pleasant and unpleasant. Some feelings are intense and others are subtle; some are long-lasting whereas others are fleeting. Certain feelings arise on a regular basis and others only on rare occasions. Some feelings are readily revealed to people and other feelings are usually hidden. Some feelings are easily tolerated, whereas other feelings are extremely difficult to endure.

The feelings accompanying traumatization add to the already diverse mix of human emotions. In order to effectively cope with the psychological impact of trauma, it is important to acknowledge your various feelings so they can be understood, accepted, and appropriately expressed. Admitting to yourself that you have unpleasant feelings does not mean that you must be resigned to feeling bad. You can learn to accept these feelings without judging them, knowing that they will pass and that they will not prevent you from being able to have pleasant emotions as well. Cooperating with these difficult feelings empowers you to move through them, whereas pushing them down saps your energy.

This art experience is designed to help you understand the diversity of your feelings and the degree to which you can acknowledge, tolerate, and express specific emotions. You will be creating a multi-layered artwork to aid in this introspective process.

Estimated Completion Time 45 - 60 minutes

Art Materials
- one sheet of 18" × 24" white drawing paper
- seven sheets of 12" × 12" wax paper
- oil pastels

Getting Started

Choose and list seven feeling words (see DESCRIBING YOUR FEELINGS on page 132), each representative of one of the following:

- a feeling you often reveal to others

- a feeling you generally keep to yourself

- a feeling that has increased in frequency or intensity since the trauma

- a feeling you wish would go away, never to return again

- a feeling you like to have

- a feeling you can live with, but one that challenges you

- a feeling you rarely experience and wish you could have more often

Artmaking Guidelines

1. Select one oil pastel color to represent each of the feelings you have listed above. Make a key for your artwork by marking the color you have chosen next to each of the feelings.

2. Represent each of the feelings by drawing lines and/or shapes with the pastel color you have chosen on separate sheets of 12" × 12" wax paper. Leave at least a 2" unused border around the edge of the wax paper.

3. Stack the pieces of wax paper in various orders, until you find the order that is most satisfactory to you.

4. Glue each piece of wax paper along the top edge to the one below it, and glue the bottom piece to the sheet of white paper.

5. Trim all paper edges as you wish.

Layered Feelings

MANAGING TRAUMATIC STRESS THROUGH ART
© SIDRAN PRESS, 1995

Written Reflections

1. List the feelings from the top layer to the bottom. List them in a vertical column on the left, allowing space between each of the feelings to describe the color, lines, and shapes representing each of the feelings and their symbolic significance.

2. Describe colors, lines, and shapes that you can see when you look at the artwork as a whole, with the layers resting on top of one another. Include the following in your description:

- What feeling is most noticeable?

- What feeling is on the top?

- What feeling is on the bottom?

- What feeling(s) are hidden?

- What feeling is the most visible toward the edges?

Layered Feelings

MANAGING TRAUMATIC STRESS
THROUGH ART
© SIDRAN PRESS, 1995

3. Notice the relationships between your feelings, by lifting each of the wax paper sheets one at a time. Comment on what you observe after lifting each sheet. How do the feelings modify or affect one another?

4. Review your responses to #2 and #3 above and consider how this artwork reflects the ways in which you experience your emotions.

5. Write about other observations and thoughts concerning these feelings. Include comments on how you acknowledge, tolerate, and express these specific feelings.

Layered
Feelings

MANAGING TRAUMATIC STRESS
THROUGH ART
© SIDRAN PRESS, 1995

13 | Mixture of Opposites

Managing the emotional pain that accompanies trauma is often one of the most difficult tasks of the coping process. During the most painful periods, you may yearn to be free and to be happy. However, it is important to remember that no one is happy all the time, and that emotional pain can be successfully managed. Accepting that you can never be totally pain-free and that the level of pain will constantly change throughout life are important steps toward healthy readjustment following trauma.

Some people who have survived trauma tend to alternate between extreme pain and extreme happiness. This experience can be likened to being on an emotional roller coaster. Finding ways to comfortably balance pain and happiness at the same time is necessary and helpful. Give yourself permission to feel your feelings whenever they arise and accept them without judging them as good or bad. Even when you are in the deepest pain, there can be moments of somewhat lighter mood states, including humor or even joy.

This art experience helps you to express pain and happiness and to explore the relationship between these two emotional states. You will create three small painting collages to explore different combinations of pain and happiness.

Estimated Completion Time 60 - 90 minutes

Art Materials

- one sheet of 18" × 24" white drawing paper cut into eight 6" × 9" pieces
- acrylic paints (brush, palette, and water)
- a spoon
- scissors
- glue

Getting Started

Write about how you experience emotional pain and happiness. Include a description of how each of these feelings affect you physically.

Artmaking Guidelines

1. Consider your state of emotional pain. What color represents this pain? Make about three teaspoons of this color, mixing together several colors, if necessary.

2. Imagine happiness. What color represents this feeling? Make about three teaspoons of this color, mixing together several colors, if necessary.

3. Mix one teaspoon of each of these two colors together. You will now have three different colors on your palette.

4. Paint two sheets of 6" × 9" paper with each of the three colors, so that you have six painted sheets of paper.

5. Allow the six painted sheets to dry.

6. Take one painted sheet of each color and cut it into four equal rectangles.

7. Visualize a simple abstract shape to represent emotional pain. Cut out three of these shapes from three of the *small* rectangles of "pain-colored" paper.

8. Visualize a simple abstract shape to represent your feeling of happiness. Cut out three of these shapes from three of the *small* rectangles of "happy-colored" paper.

9. Visualize a simple abstract shape to represent a feeling somewhere between pain and happiness. Cut out three of these shapes from three of the *small* rectangles of the remaining color of paper.

10. Place the three *large* painted sheets of paper in front of you. Place one of each of the three shapes on each of the large sheets.

11. Arrange and glue the shapes onto the three painted backgrounds.

Mixture of Opposites

MANAGING TRAUMATIC STRESS
THROUGH ART
© SIDRAN PRESS, 1995

Written Reflections

1. Look at the three collages you have completed. Arrange them in a progressive order from the "happy" background to the "pain" background. What do you notice?

2. Describe the significance of the colors and shapes that represent pain and happiness.

3. Look at the background color of the middle collage. List possible feelings that this color could represent. (See DESCRIBING YOUR FEELINGS on page 132.)

4. Observe the change in the color intensity of the shapes on the different backgrounds. The pain shape will probably appear to be more intense (stand out more) on the happy background than on the middle or pain background. The happy shape will probably appear to be more intense (stand out more) on the pain background than on the middle or happy background. Write about how this visual principle might apply to your life.

5. Write down your observations about the relationships between pain and happiness in the middle collage.

6. Decide whether you prefer one collage over the others. What does your choice say about you?

7. Spend a few minutes considering and writing about the significance to you of this series of art works.

8. Describe healthy ways you have dealt with emotional pain in the past and/or productive possibilities for the future. What will help you to "hold" both pain and happiness at the same time?

Note You may want to make an additional painting series following the above procedure but substituting different emotions:

- anger—peace
- interest—boredom
- enjoyment—displeasure
- fear—safety
- distress—calmness
- shame—pride
- hate—love

Mixture of
Opposites

MANAGING TRAUMATIC STRESS
THROUGH ART
© SIDRAN PRESS, 1995

Validating Anger

Like all emotions, anger is normal to experience and healthy to express, as long as it is done without harm to yourself or others. Anger can be a motivator, prompting people to recognize the need to make a productive change in their lives. Anger often masks the hurt from feelings of being let-down, misunderstood, attacked, or rejected. Anger is also a typical response to the injustice of traumatization. Rage, anger in its extreme form, is common among sufferers of extreme post-traumatic stress.

You may voluntarily choose to withhold anger or you may have been taught or forced to suppress your anger. One thing that intimidates people about acknowledging or expressing their anger is the fear of losing physical or emotional control. People can also be reluctant to express angry feelings for fear of hurting or repelling others. By acknowledging and attending to your anger conscientiously, you will be able to safely modulate its intensity.

This art experience allows you to explore your anger through metaphor. It also helps you to identify how to begin managing your anger, by creating a magazine picture collage.

Estimated Completion Time   45 - 60 minutes

Art Materials

- one sheet of 18" × 24" white drawing paper
- magazine pictures
- scissors
- glue

Getting Started

Take a moment to remember what it feels like to be angry; be sure to consider the physical as well as emotional signals.

Artmaking Guidelines

1. Look through magazines to find an image that can complete this statement: "My anger is like a _____." For this experience, it is more helpful to choose a picture of an object from nature or a manufactured item rather than a person or an animal.

2. Cut out the picture you have chosen.

3. Look at the picture that represents your anger and answer the following:
   - Describe its texture, weight, size, and temperature.
   - What would it feel like to hold this in your hands?
   - What sound (if any) does it make?
   - What sound(s) would you like it to make?
   - What would it say if it could speak?
   - Describe the environment in which it could be found.
   - Does it move or is it stationary?
   - If it moved, how would you describe its rhythm, speed, and style?

4. Look through magazines again and find one or more pictures that can be "helpful" to the anger image you chose.

5. Move the pictures of your "anger" and "helper" around the drawing paper until you find a meaningful arrangement.

6. Glue them to the paper.

7. Take as long as you need to allow any angry feelings that you experienced at this time to fade.

MANAGING TRAUMATIC STRESS
THROUGH ART
© SIDRAN PRESS, 1995

59

Written Reflections

1. Notice what is most visually striking to you about your artwork.

2. Describe the similarities between the picture representing anger and your feelings of anger.

3. Describe the qualities of the "helpful" picture that you chose. How could the qualities of the "helper" be of benefit to your anger image?

4. Explain any significance in the way you placed the pictures in relation to each other.

MANAGING TRAUMATIC STRESS
THROUGH ART
© SIDRAN PRESS, 1995

5. Identify what the "helpful" picture could represent in your life. How might you use this to manage your anger?

6. Consider other realistic and constructive ways to manage your anger.

7. Explore possibilities of how this anger could be useful to you. What positive changes can this anger prompt you to make?

8. Consider ways that you could assertively and respectfully express this anger.

Note You can use this exercise to explore other uncomfortable feelings, as well as pleasant feelings.

Validating
Anger

MANAGING TRAUMATIC STRESS
THROUGH ART
© SIDRAN PRESS, 1995

Imprint of Fear

Fear can be useful. It often serves as an emotional signal of real danger in our lives, helping us to protect ourselves from harm. But, fear can prevent us from engaging in productive and satisfying activities if it is excessive, unfounded, or causes us to become paralyzed. Fear is naturally intensified following trauma. Fears that may increase include those of becoming critically ill, of becoming physically or emotionally harmed by others, of being rejected or abandoned, or of going out of control. Not all fears related to trauma are exaggerated or unrealistic. For example, the fear associated with walking down a deserted street after dark is legitimate, whether or not you have ever been robbed or assaulted. Furthermore, certain smells, noises, places, and events associated with a trauma may trigger extreme levels of fear or panic. The degree of these reactions, however, may not be appropriate to the current situation.

It is important to acknowledge your fears and to understand how they relate to the trauma. Post-traumatic adjustment requires you to devise ways of reducing fear or of continuing to live productively in spite of fear.

Fears can be made tolerable in a number of ways, including:
- identifying those that are unwarranted or irrelevant to the current situation
- distinguishing between valid and unreasonable levels of fear
- determining if there is something that can be done to avert a potential problem
- accepting the fact that some fears are realistic and are an unavoidable part of contemporary life.

This art experience helps you to acknowledge your fear and to understand the effect it has on your life. You will be creating a series of monoprints to represent fear.

Estimated Completion Time 60 - 90 minutes

Art Materials

- one sheet of 18" × 24" white drawing paper cut into six 6" × 9" pieces
- acrylic paints (brushes, palette, and water)

Getting Started

1. Identify fears that have developed as a direct result of your traumatic experience.

2. List any sounds, smells, places, things, or situations that trigger high levels of fear for you.

3. Name the one thing in your life that you tend to avoid most because of fear.

4. Cite a few situations in which you feel only slightly fearful or not fearful at all.

Artmaking Guidelines

1. Choose or mix three paint colors to symbolize your feelings of fear.

2. Paint an abstract picture of fear on one 6" × 9" sheet of paper. You will be using this paper to transfer a print to another sheet of paper, so apply the paint liberally to the surface. Concern yourself primarily with making shapes or a pattern that conveys your experience of fear. You will have to work quickly so that the painting does not begin to dry before you make the print.

3. Place a clean sheet of paper on top of the wet painting.

4. Press the entire surface of the sheet with your hands, transferring paint to the inner side of the clean sheet of paper, making a print from the original.

5. Lay the print "face up" on the table. Place another sheet of clean paper on top of the print. Again, press across the surface with your hands to allow the paint to produce a second print.

6. Make a third print from the second print.

7. Repeat the printing process again, if there is enough wet paint left.

Imprint of
Fear

MANAGING TRAUMATIC STRESS
THROUGH ART
© SIDRAN PRESS, 1995

Written Reflections

1. Consider the symbolism of the colors and shapes you chose to represent fear.

2. Line the prints up in the order that you created them, with the original on the left, and the last print on the right. Notice that the intensity of the paint decreases from left to right. Describe the different levels of fear represented by each of the prints.

3. Select the print that best represents your current level of fear.

4. Think of a recent situation in which you felt fearful. Indicate the print that best represents that level of fear. Looking back on the situation and outcome, would you say your level of fear at the time was:

   ■ warranted?

   ■ excessive?

   ■ appropriate?

   ■ understated?

Imprint of
Fear

MANAGING TRAUMATIC STRESS
THROUGH ART
© SIDRAN PRESS, 1995

64

5. Identify one of your greatest fears and write about what fuels this fear.

6. Determine what issues you might have to deal with in order to lessen this fear.

7. Look at the last print in your series. If you were to decrease the level of your fear to this point, would it allow more room for other things in your life? If you felt less fear would you

- be able to feel more peace, power, or self-worth?

- begin a new activity or hobby?

- make a change in a relationship?

Be specific about what might change for *you* if you felt less fear.

Note Use oil pastels to fill in all or some of the white spaces in your last print to represent what you wrote about in WRITTEN REFLECTION #7. Repeat this art experience to explore other feelings such as anger, depression, shame, or guilt.

Imprint of
Fear

MANAGING TRAUMATIC STRESS
THROUGH ART
© SIDRAN PRESS, 1995

Shame and Guilt

People often believe they were responsible for the occurrence or outcome of the trauma they experienced, even if there was no possible alternative or escape available to them at the time. Such self-imposed judgments may lead to feelings of shame and guilt. These destructive feelings may be reinforced by non-supportive professionals, family members, or acquaintances.

Guilt derives from a sense of wrongdoing and the need for forgiveness. Shame is related to feeling embarrassed, unworthy, or defective. Both shame and guilt have a direct effect on how you perceive yourself. They may harm your ability to be comfortable with yourself and others. Shame and guilt can result in a loss of self-esteem. This is often followed by withdrawal (to avoid being seen) or aggression (to guard against the anxiety of being perceived as a bad or defective person).

Reducing trauma-related shame and guilt is a crucial and difficult part of the healing process. Accepting these feelings as a reasonable, normal response to trauma will lessen their negative impact on you. Building self-esteem can protect you from shaming messages from yourself or others. As you decrease the influence of shame and guilt, self-respect and self-esteem can grow. By acting in ways that make you feel competent and effective, doing things that are difficult and involve a challenge, getting up after you fall down, and expressing your own values and beliefs, you can enhance your sense of self-respect.

You will be creating four artworks made from oil pastel rubbings of textures in your environment. Part 1 of this art experience helps you to acknowledge identity issues associated with shame and guilt, whether they are self-imposed or imposed upon you by others. Part 2 offers a method to begin reducing shame and guilt by improving your sense of self-respect and self-worth.

Estimated Completion Time   60 - 90 minutes

Art Materials
- two sheets of 18" × 24" white drawing paper cut up into eight 9" × 12" pieces (You will be using five of these pieces in this art experience.)
- three sheets of 9" × 12" wax paper
- two figures in the APPENDIX
- oil pastels
- scissors
- iron

PART 1: FIGURING OUT SHAME AND GUILT

Getting Started

Describe how you have developed feelings of shame or guilt as a result of your traumatic experience.

Artmaking Guidelines

1. Use a gray colored oil pastel to make textural rubbing samples of several surfaces in your surroundings. To do this, place a sheet of wax paper on a textured surface (wall, floor, window screen, corrugated cardboard, sandpaper, etc.) and rub the oil pastel vigorously over the wax paper. Decide which of these textures best represents your feelings of shame or guilt.

2. Choose two or three colors of oil pastel to represent feelings of shame and/or guilt that have developed as a result of the traumatic experience.

3. Place a new sheet of wax paper on a textured surface and follow the same directions as ARTMAKING GUIDELINES #1 with one of the new colors. Place that same sheet of wax paper on another textured surface and add color to it with the second oil pastel.

4. Cut out one figure provided in the APPENDIX.

5. Position the cut-out figure in the center of a 9" × 12" sheet of white drawing paper. Do *not* glue down.

6. Turn the iron on and set it to a high temperature.

7. Place the rubbing—pastel side down—on top of the white drawing paper, being careful not to move the paper figure.

8. Sandwich the artwork between large sheets of clean paper (to protect your ironing surface and iron).

9. Transfer the rubbing to the paper by ironing the "sandwich" for about a minute, moving the iron back and forth over the surface. (The heat is sufficient to transfer the oil pastel. It is not necessary to use heavy pressure of the iron.) If you have correctly transferred the rubbing, you will now have the following:

   - a cut-out figure covered with oil pastel
   - a 9" × 12" sheet of paper with a white figure in the middle, surrounded by pastel

10. Glue the cut-out figure onto the center of a sheet of 9" × 12" white drawing paper.

Shame and
Guilt

MANAGING TRAUMATIC STRESS
THROUGH ART
© SIDRAN PRESS, 1995

Written Reflections

1. Study the two artworks for a few moments and write down your initial thoughts about each of them.

2. Discuss the significance of the colors and textures you chose to represent your shame and/or guilt.

3. Look at the artwork with the cut-out figure in the center. Write about how self-judgment has contributed to your feelings of shame and guilt.

4. Identify self-imposed "rules" that let shame and/or guilt remain strong.

5. Look at the artwork with the white figure in the center. Describe things other people have said or done that have caused you to believe that you may be responsible for the trauma or for your inability to recover from the trauma.

6. Pinpoint any other social or cultural standards that have reinforced your shame and guilt.

7. Give one or two examples of how the shame and guilt have affected your current life.

Shame and
Guilt

MANAGING TRAUMATIC STRESS
THROUGH ART
© SIDRAN PRESS, 1995

PART 2: A WORTHY FIGURE

Getting Started

1. Describe an instance or period in your life when you felt a positive sense of self-worth and self-respect.

2. Identify a couple of times when you have enhanced your self-respect by meeting a difficult challenge, standing up for your own values and beliefs, trying again after you have failed, and acting competently.

3. List events, accomplishments, or actions that provide you with a sense of self-respect and self-worth. These may include doing your best at work, taking care of your physical needs, fulfilling family responsibilities, being in school or working, and volunteering your time and talents to help others.

4. List times when others gave you positive feedback about your importance to them and their respect for you. Were you able to accept this feedback, allowing it to enhance your sense of self-worth? If not, why?

Artmaking Guidelines

1. Choose two or three oil pastel colors and textured surfaces to symbolize self-respect and self-worth.

2. Place a sheet of wax paper on a textured surface that can represent self-worth and rub the oil pastel vigorously over the wax paper. Make rubbings on the sheet of wax paper using the colors you have chosen to represent self-worth. You may choose to make the rubbings on top of one another, partially overlapping, or on separate areas of the wax paper.

3. Cut out the remaining figure provided in the APPENDIX.

4. Position the unused cut-out figure in the center of a sheet of 9" × 12" sheet of white drawing paper. Do *not* glue down.

5. Set the iron on "High" and turn it on.

6. Place the rubbing—pastel side down—on top of the white drawing paper and the cut-out figure, being careful not to move the figure.

7. Sandwich the artwork between large sheets of clean paper (to protect your ironing surface and iron).

8. Transfer the rubbing to the paper by ironing the "sandwich" for about a minute, moving the iron back and forth over the surface of the "sandwich." You do not have to use pressure to transfer the oil pastel, as the heat from the iron is sufficient to do the job. If you have correctly transferred the rubbing, you will now have:

   ■ a pastel covered cut-out figure
   ■ a 9" × 12" sheet of paper with a white figure in the middle, surrounded by pastel

9. Glue the cut-out figure onto the center of a sheet of 9" × 12" white drawing paper.

Shame and Guilt

MANAGING TRAUMATIC STRESS THROUGH ART
© SIDRAN PRESS, 1995

Written Reflections

1. Study the two artworks you completed in this part of the art experience. Write down your initial thoughts and impressions about each of them.

2. Discuss the symbolism of the colors and textures you chose to represent self-respect and worth.

3. Imagine that the positive things about you are just as valid as the negative ones. What difference would this make in your view of yourself?

4. Think of something you would enjoy doing that could also increase your sense of self-worth or self-respect. How could you go about accomplishing this?

MANAGING TRAUMATIC STRESS
THROUGH ART
© SIDRAN PRESS, 1995

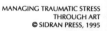

17 | *Lost and Found*

Regardless of the nature or severity of your traumatic experiences, feelings of loss will arise. These feelings are a natural reaction to actual or imagined losses that vary according to the type and impact of the trauma.

It is common to experience a loss of one or more of the following as a result of trauma:
- a sense of safety and security
- meaning and purpose in life
- physical health or body integrity
- the ability to relate effectively with others
- self-esteem or identity
- someone or something you love

Reactions to loss vary from person to person. Sometimes people do not recognize or fully experience loss, because of shock and/or denial. Denial can initially protect people from overwhelming distress and pain. As denial slowly diminishes, it gradually becomes easier to acknowledge and accept losses. Once losses are acknowledged and accepted, the process of grieving can begin.

The development of self-compassion is also important to this process. It goes hand-in-hand with the acknowledgment of painful losses. Self-compassion does not mean that you feel sorry for yourself or pity yourself, but that you recognize your suffering and can allow yourself to get the support you need. Compassion for yourself also allows you to process your losses in a healing non-destructive way. Most people who have experienced trauma will eventually reach a time when they can accept their losses and when the pain of grief fades. Some degree of sadness, however, may always remain.

This art experience helps you to validate feelings of loss related to your trauma and to increase compassion for yourself. You will be making a greeting card.

Estimated Completion Time 60 - 90 minutes

Art Materials
- one sheet of 18" × 24" white drawing paper cut into four 9" × 12" pieces
- scratch paper
- acrylic paints (brushes and water)
- a few small containers for water and paint

1. List some of the losses associated with the trauma you experienced.

2. Recall "Thinking of You" cards you have received, sent, or seen in a store.

3. Compose a sympathetic and supportive letter or poem to an imaginary person who has experienced trauma like yours.

You may want to:

■ acknowledge that the trauma occurred

■ name some of the losses

■ relay your hopes for the recipient of the card

■ offer your aid and support

Lost and Found

MANAGING TRAUMATIC STRESS
THROUGH ART
© SIDRAN PRESS, 1995

Artmaking Guidelines

1. Mix three or four comforting colors of paint in separate containers. Thin the paints with water so they are the consistency of watercolors.

2. Experiment with the colors on scratch paper:

   - apply the color to dry paper
   - apply the color to wet paper
   - place two colors next to each other on wet paper and allow them to merge

3. Fold a sheet of 9" × 12" drawing paper in half. Cut it to the size and shape of a greeting card. (Substitute a blank greeting card for the folded paper, if you wish.)

4. Create a comforting or hopeful image on the front of the card. This image can be abstract or realistic.

5. Decide if you want a phrase on the front of the card such as "Thinking of You" and add it, if you so desire.

6. Transcribe your completed letter or poem (from "GETTING STARTED" # 3) to the inside of the card when the watercolors have dried. Use all the space you need, including additional paper if necessary.

7. Make an envelope for your card from white drawing paper.

Written Reflections

1. Describe your thoughts and feelings while making the card.

MANAGING TRAUMATIC STRESS
THROUGH ART
© SIDRAN PRESS, 1995

2. Describe any changes in your awareness of personal loss.

3. Place your card in a stamped envelope that is addressed to you. Mail the card to yourself. Write about how you think you will feel when you receive and read the card. Compare these ideas to how you actually feel when you receive the card.

4. Display the card where you will see it regularly once you receive it in the mail. Later, you may want to place it in the Comfort Box that you created in ART EXPERIENCE #6.

5. Consider other ways you might continue to acknowledge your losses, develop self-compassion, and offer aid and support to yourself.

Lost and Found

MANAGING TRAUMATIC STRESS
THROUGH ART
© SIDRAN PRESS, 1995

18 | Mind and Heart

Effective functioning requires attention to both feelings and logical thought. Each of us has a tendency to over-rely on either thought or feeling when under stress; we may think of that as our strength but, out of balance, it could actually be our weakness. When people become disconnected from their emotions, they tend to rely primarily on their intellect to make decisions and inform their daily actions. Such people are often perceived to be cold-hearted, rigid, or inhuman. Post-traumatic emotional numbing can have this effect on you. On the other hand, when people become overwhelmed by their feelings, their decisions and actions may be guided by impulsiveness. Such people are often perceived to be irritable, hysterical, or temperamental. Post-traumatic emotional flooding can have this effect on you, too.

Decisions and actions based primarily on either emotions or intellect usually have positive short-term results, but negative long-term consequences. Balancing and integrating careful thought and heartfelt emotion can enhance your life skills and help you develop a more effective functioning style.

This art experience encourages you to learn and practice effective blending of your rational thought with sincere feeling. You will be creating two abstract oil pastel drawings to combine into a unique shape symbolizing a style of response that unites thinking and feeling.

Estimated Completion Time   45 - 60 minutes

Art Materials

- one sheet of 18" × 24" white drawing paper cut into four 9" × 12" pieces (You will be using three pieces of 9" × 12" paper in this art experience.)
- oil pastels

1. Remember a situation in which you took action based solely on emotion.

2. Remember a situation in which you took action based solely on intellect, with no consideration of your feelings.

Mind and
Heart

MANAGING TRAUMATIC STRESS
THROUGH ART
© SIDRAN PRESS, 1995

79

Artmaking Guidelines

1. Visualize a shape to represent the overwhelming feelings that can govern your responses and behaviors. Draw this shape on the first sheet of drawing paper using oil pastels. Embellish or refine your picture, using lines, shapes, and colors to fully express this state of mind.

2. Visualize a shape to represent your responses that are characterized primarily by intellectualization and emotional detachment. Draw this image on the second sheet of drawing paper using oil pastels. Embellish or refine your picture as necessary to accurately illustrate this state of mind.

3. Place your two drawings side by side and compare their graphic qualities and characteristics.

4. Imagine a response that combines careful thought *and* heartfelt emotion. Visualize a shape to represent this combination. You may use characteristics from your previous images if you wish. Draw this composite image on the third sheet of drawing paper using oil pastels. Embellish or refine this picture as necessary to reflect this unification.

Written Reflections

1. Describe each of your three pictures in words, phrases, or sentences. (See DESCRIBING YOUR ART on page 135.)

2. Consider how the above description is parallel to responses that are strictly emotional, strictly intellectual, or a combination of the two.

3. Identify an issue in your current life that requires action. Using the three symbols you created, determine actions that would come out of an emotional response, an intellectual response, and a combined response. Which response would prove most effective?

Mind and
Heart

MANAGING TRAUMATIC STRESS
THROUGH ART
© SIDRAN PRESS, 1995

SECTION THREE

Functioning and Being in the World

19 | Self-Image

Your self-image is partially defined by your life experiences. Consequently, the trauma you experienced, regardless of its nature and severity, can affect your self-perception.

If you experienced early trauma, such as emotional, physical, or sexual abuse, personal losses, illness, or accidents, your self-image may be largely defined by these events. Recent traumatic events, such as divorce, the death of a loved one, or a violation of your physical integrity, might lower your self-esteem, and increase your emotional fragility and vulnerability.

While it may not be possible to fully separate your traumatic experience from your sense of self, it is necessary to evaluate how it might distort your self-perception. Traumatic experiences in your recent past may result in faulty logic, such as "Bad things always happen to me, I must deserve it," or "It is all my fault that this happened." Early trauma (such as childhood abuse or extended illnesses) may lead you to believe, "I am getting hurt because I am a bad person." Trauma may also cause you to see yourself as unstable, abnormal, debilitated, helpless, unattractive, or worthless.

The process of redefining yourself in healthier, more affirming terms involves many steps. Separating yourself from the trauma involves learning to say to yourself, "The trauma is something that happened to me; it is *not* me." One good way to do this is to try to extend the same support and forgiveness to yourself that you might show a friend.

You will be creating two photocopy collages to represent current and transformed self-perceptions. Part 1 of this art experience helps you to explore your current self-image as it is influenced by trauma. Part 2 asks you to envision what your self-image could be if not extensively influenced by the trauma.

Note THIS EXPERIENCE REQUIRES ACCESS TO A PHOTOCOPIER.

Estimated Completion Time 60 - 90 minutes

Art Materials
- one sheet of 18" × 24" white drawing paper cut up into four 9" × 12" pieces (You will be using two pieces of 9" × 12" paper for this art experience.)
- two photocopies of a recent photo of yourself (you may wish to enlarge or reduce the original photo)
- frames in the APPENDIX
- colored pencils
- scissors
- glue

Getting Started

Consider ways that trauma has affected your view of yourself. This may include perceptions of your physical, emotional, and intellectual characteristics.

Artmaking Guidelines

1. Select one of the frames in the APPENDIX to symbolically represent your trauma.

2. Cut the frame out and place it on a sheet of 9" × 12" white drawing paper.

3. Place the photocopy of the picture of yourself inside the frame. If you enlarged or reduced the picture, choose a size that you find compatible with the frame.

4. Glue your frame and photocopy onto the drawing paper.

5. Trim around the outside edges of your frame to remove any excess drawing paper.

6. Choose one or more colored pencil(s) to symbolize how the trauma has affected your self-image.

7. Color the photocopy of your photo.

Self-Image

MANAGING TRAUMATIC STRESS
THROUGH ART
© SIDRAN PRESS, 1995

85

Written Reflections

1. Look at the photocopy of your photo. Think about the reason you chose it for this art experience.

2. Now consider the frame you chose. What initially drew you to that particular design?

3. Discuss how the features of your frame relate to your trauma.

4. List the colored pencils you picked and their symbolic meaning for you. Is there any particular significance in the way you applied them to your image?

5. Discuss how it feels to see a tangible image that reflects how the trauma has "framed" your sense of self.

PART 2: A NEW FRAME OF REFERENCE

Getting Started

1. Observe the artwork you completed in Part 1 of this art experience. Look at the artwork as if it were a picture of someone else.

2. Imagine the feelings you would have for this person if you were told what had happened to him or her.

Artmaking Guidelines

1. Select a frame that could transform this person's self-image in a positive way, one that is not solely determined by the trauma.

2. Cut this frame out and place it on a sheet of 9" × 12" white drawing paper.

3. Place a photocopy of the photo inside this frame. If you enlarged or reduced this photo, choose a size that you find compatible with the frame.

4. Glue the frame and photocopy onto the drawing paper.

5. Trim around the outside edges of the frame to remove any excess photocopy paper.

6. Choose one or more colored pencil(s) to symbolically reflect the changes in how this person might view him or herself.

7. Color the photocopy with colored pencils to reflect this transformation.

Self-
Image

MANAGING TRAUMATIC STRESS
THROUGH ART
© SIDRAN PRESS, 1995

Written Reflections

1. Determine what initially influenced your choice of one frame over the others.

2. Discuss the various features of this frame and their significance to you.

3. List the colors of pencils you picked and their symbolic meaning for you. Is there any particular significance in the way you applied them to the image?

4. Compare the two artworks you created in this art experience. How did your self-image change in relation to the frame around it?

5. If you continue to retain the image of yourself within the new frame, what difference could this make in your life?

6. Consider what stops you from continually seeing yourself in the new frame.

7. Identify one small step you could take that could move you toward your preferred self-image.

MANAGING TRAUMATIC STRESS
THROUGH ART
© SIDRAN PRESS, 1995

20 | *Role Quilt*

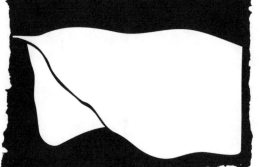

Traumatic experiences almost always produce changes in the ways people perform various roles in their daily lives. Some roles are modified, while others may be discontinued or new ones created. Both at-home and work roles may be changed as a result of trauma. Some role changes are necessary for practical reasons. For example, following the sudden death of a partner, the remaining partner may need to work more for financial reasons. At other times, role changes might provide temporary relief from traumatic stress, but they might cause additional stress if sustained for a long time. For instance, a person who has been sexually assaulted may stop being physically intimate with a partner. This may be a temporary necessity to reduce distress, but will be harmful to the relationship if continued indefinitely. Exploring the ways traumatic stress has influenced your various roles can provide useful insights into your identity. You may also become aware of wants or needs related to potential role changes.

This art experience provides a way to identify and explore the various roles you play in your current life and the ways they have been affected by trauma. You will be creating a miniature paper quilt to represent these roles.

Estimated Completion Time 60 - 90 minutes

Art Materials

- one sheet of 18" × 24" white drawing paper
- assorted novelty papers (these might include wrapping papers, handmade papers, foils, paper bags, facial tissue, paper napkins or towels, sandpaper, printed envelopes, pages out of magazines or newspapers)
- ruler
- pencil
- scissors
- glue

Getting Started

Make a list of your current life roles. Consider the following:

- family roles: mother, father, son, daughter, sister, brother, husband, wife, partner

- other interpersonal relationships: friend, lover, companion, co-worker, caretaker, mentor, supervisor, employee

- job, vocation, student status

- leisure or recreational roles: artist, musician, runner, walker, tv viewer, reader, movie-goer, sports participant or fan, dancer, exerciser, writer

- other roles: patient, client, consumer, spiritual or philosophical devotee

Role Quilt

MANAGING TRAUMATIC STRESS
THROUGH ART
© SIDRAN PRESS, 1995

Artmaking Guidelines

1. Select a different type of paper (using those you have collected for this art experience) to represent each of the roles that you identified above in GETTING STARTED.

2. Cut five 1 1/2" squares from each of the papers.

3. Arrange these squares into one large rectangular form in the center of a sheet of 18" × 24" paper. Play with different arrangements until you sense that the overall design is "right." You do not need to incorporate all of the squares into the quilt design, but include at least one square representing each role.

4. Glue the squares to the paper.

5. Select paper to use as a border around the quilt squares. This paper may be the same as, or different from, the ones you used for the squares.

6. Cut the border paper into strips and glue them around the edges of the rectangle.

Written Reflections

1. Describe any symbolism in the color and texture of the papers you chose.

2. Write about how the quilt's border relates to your identity and your life.

3. Consider the following questions for each of the roles that are represented in your quilt (use a separate sheet of paper for your responses, if needed):

■ Has your ability to perform the role improved or declined since the trauma? Why?

■ In what other ways did the trauma change that role?

■ Was the role created as a result of the trauma? Why?

■ Has a change in that role been an improvement or has it had a negative effect on your sense of well-being?

4. Describe any of your roles that were discontinued because of the indirect or direct effects of the trauma.

5. Note one role change you would like to make in the future.

Role Quilt

MANAGING TRAUMATIC STRESS
THROUGH ART
© SIDRAN PRESS, 1995

Life Skills

Coping mechanisms help us to meet the challenges in our lives. They allow us to survive almost any situation with which we are confronted, including major trauma. To reduce the internal tension resulting from trauma, people learn to choose behaviors that work for the moment. Some common coping methods that may follow a traumatic experience include disconnection from emotions, denial of the extent of the trauma, substance abuse, unhealthy eating habits, secrecy and withdrawal from others, perfectionism, rigid emotional or physical boundaries, and heightened sensitivity to environmental stimuli. The coping mechanisms that any person uses are related to individual needs and behavioral styles.

Coping mechanisms are necessary to survive trauma, but it is important to assess their impact on your sense of self and your ability to function. Not all coping behaviors are the best or healthiest alternatives. Some will hinder your ability to function, undermine the quality of your life, and negatively affect your identity if used for extended periods of time after the traumatic situation or event.

Seeking the connections between your traumatic experience and the self-defeating behaviors you use that temporarily ease the pain enables you to identify and choose healthier options. These options or life skills may include appropriate cautiousness; emotional awareness and safe expression; clear and flexible boundaries; responsible assertiveness; recognition of both short- and long-term consequences of behaviors; and development of supportive connections to others while maintaining a sense of autonomy. These life skills are best learned one small step at a time. They are the inner workings of your new wellness system.

You will create two collages with images that symbolize coping mechanisms and skills. Part 1 of this art experience asks you to represent the coping mechanisms you used to survive the period since your trauma. Part 2 helps you to identify other healthier coping skills that are life-enhancing.

Estimated Completion Time 60 - 90 minutes

Art Materials
- two sheets of 18" × 24" white drawing paper
- magazine pictures
- scissors
- glue
- tape

PART 1: BARELY COPING MECHANISM

Getting Started

1. List the behaviors you developed to help you cope after you became traumatized.

2. Explain how these coping mechanisms have affected your lifestyle and your ability to function.

Life Skills

MANAGING TRAUMATIC STRESS
THROUGH ART
© SIDRAN PRESS, 1995

Artmaking Guidelines

1. Look through the magazines, select and cut out five to eight images to symbolize your various post-traumatic coping behaviors (as described in GETTING STARTED #1).

2. Imagine a machine made from the magazine pictures you chose. Draw the simplest possible outline of your invented machine on a sheet of 18" × 24" paper. Leave enough blank space within the machine's outline for attaching its parts (the images you chose in step one).

3. Choose one or more of the magazine pictures to represent how the coping mechanisms that you just identified have affected your lifestyle and ability to function. (Refer to your responses to GETTING STARTED #2.) These magazine pictures will represent the output or product of your machine.

4. Choose one or more of the magazine pictures to represent the experiences in your life that caused you to respond with ineffective coping behaviors. These images will function as raw materials that will be transformed in your machine.

5. Place all of your images on the paper and arrange them according to their functions—machine parts within the drawn outline, raw material(s) at the loading point, and product(s) at the exit point.

6. Glue the images to the paper, adding any pertinent details to the machine. You may wish to connect parts by drawing lines, tubes, wires, rods, cogs, wheels, belts, or electronic mechanisms between them.

7. Embellish the picture's background as you wish.

Written Reflections

1. Describe the appearance and workings of your machine. What is the overall size and shape of the machine? Is it large or small, vertical or horizontal, simple or complicated, quiet or noisy? Do its parts move, blink, light up, spin, or change in anyway?

Life Skills

MANAGING TRAUMATIC STRESS
THROUGH ART
© SIDRAN PRESS, 1995

2. Explain the input(s) and output(s) of your machine. In what way do the images you chose symbolize the qualities of your trauma or lifestyle?

3. Explain how the machine parts represent your coping techniques. How do they interrelate?

4. Discuss the significance of any background elements in your picture.

5. Consider the effectiveness of your coping mechanisms in regard to your daily life.

6. Note the unproductive effects of your current coping mechanisms on your daily life.

Life Skills

MANAGING TRAUMATIC STRESS
THROUGH ART
© SIDRAN PRESS, 1995

PART 2: WELL-OILED MACHINE

Getting Started

1. List several new skills you would like to develop that would enable you to manage your stress in a healthier, more productive way.

2. Explain how these changes might affect your ability to cope with daily stress.

3. Imagine that there is a second machine made out of parts that represent new skills. If your first machine's product served as the raw material for this machine, what might the new product be?

Artmaking Guidelines

1. Place another sheet of 18" × 24" paper next to your first machine collage, on the edge closest to the image that represents the output. Tape the sheets of paper together on their back sides, making sure that the paper edges have no gap between them.

2. Select and cut out five to eight images from magazines to symbolize the new skills you would like to develop. (Remember to refer to your responses to GETTING STARTED #1.)

3. Choose one or more images to represent the output(s) or product(s) this machine is designed to make.

4. Draw a simple outline of your modified machine on the clean sheet of paper. Be sure to leave adequate space within the machine's outline for attaching all of its parts.

5. Place all of your images on the paper and arrange them in a way that has meaning for you within the machine's outline. Place the product image at the exit point of the second machine.

6. Glue the pictures to the paper, adding any pertinent details to the machine or background of the picture, as you did with the first machine collage.

Life Skills

MANAGING TRAUMATIC STRESS
THROUGH ART
© SIDRAN PRESS, 1995

Written Reflections

1. Describe the appearance and workings of your new machine.

2. Describe the modifications that you made in creating your new machine.

   ■ What do the new parts represent?

   ■ How do they interrelate with each other and the original parts?

3. Explain the output of your machine. How might this image represent changes in your daily attitudes and/or actions?

4. Discuss the significance of any background elements in your picture.

5. Study the transformation of raw materials from the first machine through the second machine. How would you characterize this process in relation to your personal experiences?

6. Identify the potential difference in your quality of life if you implemented the changes illustrated in your second collage. What will be the first step you could take toward making these changes?

Life Skills

MANAGING TRAUMATIC STRESS
THROUGH ART
© SIDRAN PRESS, 1995

22 | *Environmental Protection*

Everyone inhabits a variety of environments; home, neighborhood, school, and work are usually the ones in which the most time is spent. Gone is the time when these places can be assumed to be safe and secure. Domestic violence in the home, crime and assault in public spaces, and problems at school and work pose challenges to the young and old alike. To some, security means double-bolting their windows and doors. But security can also refer to your sense of psychological freedom and sanctuary within relationships.

Since safety and security are strongly influenced by a sense of personal power and control, traumatic or stressful experiences can result in perceived helplessness that can be seriously disempowering.

To break the cycle of anxiety and dread that follows certain negative experiences, it is helpful to evaluate the environment(s) in which you live. This means making a survey of safety and security factors to assess what is reassuring as well as what remains problematic or troublesome. Although it is impossible to live in a perfectly stress-free environment, calm and comfort should nonetheless outweigh fear and insecurity. If this is not the case, you may wish to consider making changes in your circumstances.

You will be creating two painted collages to represent part of your present environment and a possible change in this environment. Part 1 of this art experience helps you explore and evaluate the qualities of your environment, and how they influence your physical and emotional well-being. Part 2 provides a problem-solving method to identify ways of changing troublesome aspects in your environment.

Estimated Completion Time 90 - 120 minutes

Art Materials
- scratch paper
- two sheets of 18" × 24" white drawing paper
- one sheet of 18" × 24" white drawing paper cut into two 12" × 18" pieces
- acrylic paints (brushes, palette, and water)
- pen or pencil
- scissors
- glue

Getting Started

1. Make a list of the different places where you spend time during a typical week. These might include the locations where you live, work, volunteer, study, spend leisure time, or visit with other people.

2. Choose one of the places on your list. Describe the various elements in this environment, including the physical surroundings and the emotional atmosphere.

Environmental
Protection

MANAGING TRAUMATIC STRESS
THROUGH ART
© SIDRAN PRESS, 1995

Artmaking Guidelines

1. Practice making assorted types of brushstrokes with one color of paint on scratch paper. You may want to try the following:

- different sizes of brushes
- using the tip of the brush
- using the side of the brush
- quick and slow brush strokes
- long and short brush strokes
- straight, curving, and angular brush strokes
- high-pressure and low-pressure brush strokes

2. Read the notes you wrote in GETTING STARTED #2. Imagine what colors could best represent the environment you have chosen. Are they bright, dull, dark, light, or a combination of these?

3. Paint an abstract background on a sheet of 18" × 24" white drawing paper, using various types of brushstrokes to represent the different aspects of your environment.

4. Put this painting aside to dry.

5. Trace the outlines of both your right and left feet on a 12" × 18" sheet of white drawing paper.

6. Cut out these footprints.

7. Imagine yourself standing in the environment you painted. What color(s) could best represent how you would feel? Are these color(s) bright, dull, dark, light, or a combination of these?

8. Paint your footprints to reflect how you would feel in this environment. Allow the paint to dry before proceeding to the next step.

9. Place the footprints on the painting, positioning them in a variety of different arrangements. You might try placing them together or apart, putting one in front of the other, placing them toward the center of the painting or at the edges of the painting.

10. Glue your footprints to the surface when you have chosen the most satisfactory arrangement.

Environmental
Protection

MANAGING TRAUMATIC STRESS
THROUGH ART
© SIDRAN PRESS, 1995

Written Reflections

1. Describe the symbolism of the colors and brushstrokes in the background of your collage.

2. Comment on what the footprint color symbolizes.

3. Consider the significance of the placement of the footprints. (For example, could the position represent feeling enjoyment, being stuck, feeling out of place, being ready to enter or leave, being uncomfortable, feeling at ease, taking a stand?)

4. Record possible reasons for the placement of your footprints near specific sections of your collage.

5. List the elements of this environment that enhance your physical and emotional well-being and offer you comfort, support, and/or protection.

6. List the negative aspects of this environment that adversely affect your physical and emotional well-being.

7. Write about different outcomes of staying in this environment for a long period of time.

8. Consider the relationship of this environment to other past or present environments.

9. Consider the following alternatives to improve protection and safety:
   - spend less time in this environment
   - spend more time in this environment
   - physically leave this environment
   - find better ways to cope with this environment
   - explore ways to change the environment

Environmental
Protection

MANAGING TRAUMATIC STRESS
THROUGH ART
© SIDRAN PRESS, 1995

103

PART 2: STEPPING INTO THE FUTURE

Getting Started

1. Describe one problematic aspect in the environment that you painted in Part 1.

2. Devise a goal designed to address this problem by completing the following sentence: In order to make this environment more protective, supportive, satisfactory, and safe, I could

3. Consider the physical and emotional changes in your environment if you were to accomplish this goal.

Artmaking Guidelines

1. Paint an abstract background on a sheet of 18" × 24" white drawing paper to depict your environment as if your goal has been accomplished.

2. Put this painting aside to dry.

3. Trace your feet on a 12" × 18" sheet of white drawing paper.

4. Cut out your footprints.

5. Paint these footprints to indicate how you would feel if you were standing in the transformed environment you painted. Allow the paint to dry before proceeding to the next step.

6. Arrange your footprints on the surface of the painting in a meaningful way. Glue them to the surface.

Environmental
Protection

MANAGING TRAUMATIC STRESS
THROUGH ART
© SIDRAN PRESS, 1995

Written Reflections

1. Place this collage next to the collage you completed earlier in Part 1. Describe the similarities and differences between the two.

2. List a few ways that you might move toward achievement of your chosen goal in the transformed environment.

3. Write down pros and cons of each alternative listed above in #2.

4. Choose the alternative that seems to be the best at this time. Record the first step that you could take toward reaching your goal.

Note You may want to complete this art experience for other environments you frequent.

Environmental
Protection

MANAGING TRAUMATIC STRESS
THROUGH ART
© SIDRAN PRESS, 1995

Interpersonal Boundaries

Boundaries set the limit for what people allow in and what they allow out. Healthy boundaries enable people to maintain a sense of safety and comfort, emotionally, physically, and sexually. They allow you to interact with others in effective and beneficial ways. Internal boundaries remind you that you are not responsible for other people's responses and they are not responsible for yours. External boundaries act as healthy physical parameters that prevent others from entering your private space and discourage you from entering theirs.

If you were unable to form healthy, intact boundaries as a child due to trauma and/or dysfunction in your family, you may have difficulty feeling safe and comfortable anywhere or with anyone. When trauma occurs later in life, you may find that certain of your boundaries need mending or adjusting, particularly during periods of distress. When a boundary fails to do its job, you are left unprotected. Conversely, a boundary that does its job too well prevents others from getting close to you.

This art experience asks you to survey your personal boundaries. By creating two drawings, you will be assessing trauma's impact on the effectiveness of your boundaries and exploring ways you can improve your boundaries in the future.

Estimated Completion Time 60 - 90 minutes

Art Materials

- one sheet of 18" × 24" white drawing paper cut into two 12" × 18" pieces
- lead pencil, colored pencils, or oil pastels

PART 1: BARRIERS AND BROKEN BOUNDARIES

Getting Started

1. Comment on the condition and characteristics of your current boundaries. Are they nonexistent, damaged, broken, intact, flexible, severe, or inconsistent?

2. Consider which characteristics of your current boundaries have been changed or determined by the trauma you experienced.

3. Describe the condition of your boundaries before the trauma.

Artmaking Guidelines

1. Use your imagination to create a figure to represent yourself and draw it in the center of a sheet of 12" × 18" white drawing paper. The figure can be represented by an abstract shape, a cartoon, a stick figure, or it can be realistic.

2. Draw your current boundaries around the image of yourself. You may want to depict your boundaries by using lines (thick, thin, connected, or broken) or metaphoric images (walls, fences, forcefields, or bubbles).

Interpersonal
Boundaries

MANAGING TRAUMATIC STRESS
THROUGH ART
© SIDRAN PRESS, 1995

Written Reflections

1. Describe the picture of your boundaries and how it represents their condition and characteristics.

2. Comment on whether you notice any significance in the way you represented yourself within your boundaries.

3. Consider how you usually feel within these boundaries. Do you feel safe, unsafe, protected, exposed, vulnerable, or isolated?

4. Write about how you would have visually depicted the condition of your boundaries before the trauma.

Interpersonal
Boundaries

MANAGING TRAUMATIC STRESS
THROUGH ART
© SIDRAN PRESS, 1995

PART 2: BUILDING BETTER BOUNDARIES

Getting Started

Examine your first boundary drawing and consider ways you would like your boundaries to change for increased comfort and safety. You might think about the need for additions, such as windows, doors, or gates, or the need to mend a broken fence or a hole in a wall.

Artmaking Guidelines

1. Use your imagination to create a figure to represent yourself and draw it in the center of a sheet of 12" × 18" white drawing paper. Again, the figure can be an abstract shape, a cartoon, a stick figure, or a more realistic rendition.

2. Draw the boundaries you would like to have around an image of yourself. You may choose to add to or subtract from the boundary image you made in Part 1 or you may opt to depict it in an entirely different manner.

Interpersonal
Boundaries

MANAGING TRAUMATIC STRESS
THROUGH ART
© SIDRAN PRESS, 1995

Written Reflections

1. Describe the picture of your desired boundaries and how it reflects their qualities.

2. Explain any significance in the way you portrayed yourself within these boundaries. Did this image change within these new boundaries?

MANAGING TRAUMATIC STRESS
THROUGH ART
© SIDRAN PRESS, 1995

3. Consider how you might feel within these healthier boundaries. Would you feel safe, protected, accessible, or comfortable?

4. Write about how your current relationships would be affected by these new boundaries.

MANAGING TRAUMATIC STRESS
THROUGH ART
© SIDRAN PRESS, 1995

24 | *Your Level Best*

Your functioning level can vary greatly on an hour-to-hour or day-to-day basis, depending on external circumstances and your attitude, health, and skills. Trauma, too, can affect the quality of your functioning. When you are unable to function it may seem as if the trauma is affecting everything about your life; at other times you may find that traumatic stress fades from your consciousness, allowing you to function at your best. In fact, there is a wide range of functioning levels between these extremes.

It is important to monitor the level of your functioning so that you can choose to have more control over your post-traumatic symptoms and the quality of your life. When you notice that you are not functioning well, you can determine the contributing factors and take corrective action. When you are doing your best (emotionally or otherwise), notice what has contributed to this state and choose to develop these strengths or increase these factors, instead of just putting up with whatever symptoms come your way. Although a traumatic event or situation can never be erased from your life history, the degree to which it negatively affects your everyday thoughts, feelings, and actions can be lessened. With better awareness of your functioning level you can make choices to act in more effective, productive, and satisfying ways.

You will be exploring the different degrees to which post-traumatic symptoms affect your functioning by creating three collages from colored construction paper. You will also be identifying short-term goals relating to your overall level of functioning.

Estimated Completion Time 90 - 120 minutes

Art Materials
- assorted colors of construction paper
- pencil
- scissors
- glue

1. Think of a recent situation in which the aftereffects of trauma prevented you from functioning adequately.

2. Think of a recent situation in which the aftereffects of trauma had little or no effect whatsoever on your ability to function.

3. Think of a recent situation in which post-traumatic symptoms had a moderate impact on your level of functioning. (For example, you could function adequately, but with great difficulty.)

Your Level
Best

MANAGING TRAUMATIC STRESS
THROUGH ART
© SIDRAN PRESS, 1995

Artmaking Guidelines

1. Choose a different color of construction paper to represent each of the following items and cut the paper to the corresponding specifications:

- your post-traumatic symptoms (two sheets of 9" × 12" paper, one sheet of 5" × 12" paper)
- yourself (two sheets of 9" × 12" paper)
- sky (two sheets of 9" × 12" paper)
- earth (one sheet of 5" × 12" paper)

2. Create the first artwork:

   a. Imagine the posture of a figure that could represent what it is like when you are overwhelmed by your post-traumatic symptoms and unable to function.

   b. Draw an outline of this figure on one of the sheets of 9" × 12" colored paper you chose to represent *yourself* and cut it out. (Make this figure approximately 6" in height—if it were standing. You may, however, chose to make this figure sitting, or lying, or bending over in some way.)

   c. Place this figure on one of the sheets of 9" × 12" colored paper you chose to represent your *post-traumatic symptoms* and glue it down.

3. Create the second artwork:

   a. Construct a background by gluing the sheet of 5" × 12" colored paper you chose to represent your *post-traumatic symptoms* onto the bottom portion of one of the sheets of colored paper representing the *sky*.

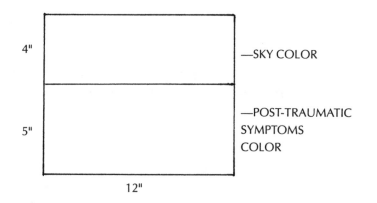

   b. Imagine the posture of a figure that could represent what it is like when the trauma has a moderate effect on your functioning.

   c. Draw an outline of this figure on one of the sheets of colored paper you chose to represent *yourself* and cut it out.

   d. Place this figure on the background you created in step 3a and glue it down.

Your Level
Best

MANAGING TRAUMATIC STRESS
THROUGH ART
© SIDRAN PRESS, 1995

114

4. Create the third artwork:

    a. Construct a background by gluing the sheet of colored paper you chose to represent the *earth* onto the bottom portion of the second sheet of colored paper representing the *sky*.

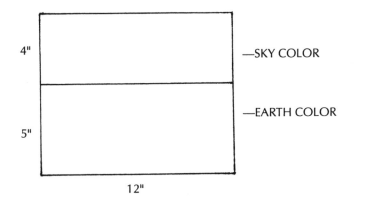

    b. Imagine the posture of a figure that could represent what it is like for you to function when your post-traumatic symptoms have little or no effect on your functioning.

    c. Draw an outline of this figure on one of the sheets of colored paper you chose to represent *yourself* and cut it out.

    d. Imagine a shape that could represent your post-traumatic symptoms. Draw this shape on the second sheet of 9" × 12" colored paper you chose to represent your *post-traumatic symptoms* and cut it out.

    e. Arrange the figure and trauma shapes on the background you created in 4a and glue them down.

Your Level
Best

MANAGING TRAUMATIC STRESS
THROUGH ART
© SIDRAN PRESS, 1995

Written Reflections

1. Describe why you chose each of the colors to represent

- your post-traumatic symptoms

- yourself

- sky

- earth

2. Line up the artworks in the order that you created them. Look at each of your collages and answer the following questions:

- What is this figure thinking?

- What is this figure feeling?

- What is this figure doing?

- What is this figure unable to do?

3. Look at the artwork that shows what it is like when the trauma has no effect on your ability to function. How are things different when the symptoms are absent? What does this difference suggest?

MANAGING TRAUMATIC STRESS
THROUGH ART
© SIDRAN PRESS, 1995

4. Estimate what proportion of your life you spend functioning at each of the three levels depicted by the collages.

5. Identify how you would like to change the balance of this functioning in the upcoming year. What differences in your behavior, thinking, and feelings would indicate that you have reached this goal?

6. Identify the first step you can take toward achieving this change in level of overall functioning. What has previously prevented you from taking this step? When, where, and how will you take this step?

7. Think of one particular aspect of your life that has been negatively affected by trauma. What would be the first sign of your improvement in regard to functioning?

Note You may want to create positive statements based on your responses to #5 and #6, make a voice bubble or thought balloon to enclose this statement, and add it to the appropriate collage.

Your Level
Best

MANAGING TRAUMATIC STRESS
THROUGH ART
© SIDRAN PRESS, 1995

25 | *Relationships*

Stress and trauma can disrupt the way you relate to other people. For example, early life trauma may hinder your capacity to form connections with others. Since child abuse typically occurs within the context of a care-giving relationship, the child's concept of relationships and their meaning may become seriously impaired; an abused child is unlikely to see relationships as safe or life-enhancing. Children who have experienced the loss of a caretaker may have difficulty forming connections because of their fear of abandonment. People who are assaulted, either as children or adults, often experience difficulty with physical intimacy. When trauma occurs in adulthood, people may find their relationships become strained or broken. For instance, those who remain physically impaired after a trauma may be overcome with depression, see themselves as unattractive or compromised, and withdraw from others.

It is important to keep in mind that healthy connections with others can help you replenish your internal resources when they have been depleted by traumatic stress; provide a sense of being needed; give purpose to your life; and allow you to experience the warmth, caring, and playfulness that can exist between human beings. It is also important to remember that you can remain responsibly independent and effectively interdependent at the same time; you can meet your needs through your own efforts and also channel your efforts, talents, and abilities into collaboration with other people to achieve beneficial, fulfilling results.

You will be creating two collages. The first will help you examine what may be hindering your ability to connect with others. The second will help you to explore important factors in connecting with others and what you need to begin that process.

Estimated Completion Time 90 - 120 minutes

Art Materials
- one sheet of 18" × 24" white or colored paper cut into two 12" × 18" pieces
- hand images in the APPENDIX
- magazine pictures and words
- scissors
- glue

PART 1: MISSED CONNECTIONS

Getting Started

1. Think about the various important relationships in your life. You might wish to review ART EXPERIENCE #5, Support Net.

2. List your relationships that have changed in terms of connectedness (mutual or one-way) and make brief notes regarding the circumstances.

Artmaking Guidelines

1. Choose one of the hand images in the APPENDIX to represent yourself and one or more hand images to represent others.

2. Cut out the hand images.

3. Look through magazines to find images and/or words that communicate factors that prevent you from connecting with people.

4. Cut out the magazine images and words.

5. Choose suitable color(s) for the background of your collage.

6. Arrange the hands and images on the background in a way that best communicates what you want the picture to symbolize about your connections with others.

7. Glue the hands, images, and words to the background page.

Relationships

MANAGING TRAUMATIC STRESS
THROUGH ART
© SIDRAN PRESS, 1995

Written Reflections

1. Describe the significance of each image you chose.

2. Comment on the significance of the background color(s).

3. Note what is symbolic about the arrangement of the hands and images on the paper.

4. Consider which images represent the more difficult barriers.

MANAGING TRAUMATIC STRESS
THROUGH ART
© SIDRAN PRESS, 1995

Getting Started

1. Describe why you want to be connected to others.

2. List possible benefits of being connected to people following your traumatic experience.

3. Describe types of people that attract you.

4. List ways you connect with people. For instance, do you find that you connect with people who have similar interests, age, or work?

Relationships

MANAGING TRAUMATIC STRESS
THROUGH ART
© SIDRAN PRESS, 1995

Artmaking Guidelines

1. Choose one or more images of the joined hands in the APPENDIX that represent the way you would like to connect with others.

2. Cut out the hand images.

3. Search through magazines to find pictures and/or words that represent what you need to form connections with others and the benefits you can receive from connecting.

4. Cut out images and words.

5. Choose suitable color(s) for the background of your collage.

6. Arrange the hands and images on the background in a way that best communicates what you want the picture to mean.

7. Glue the hands, images, and words to the background.

Written Reflections

1. Describe the significance of each image you chose.

2. Comment on the significance of the arrangement of the composition.

Relationships

MANAGING TRAUMATIC STRESS
THROUGH ART
© SIDRAN PRESS, 1995

3. Explain the meaning of the background color.

4. Choose the image on the collage that shows what your most important need is at this time to allow you to begin to connect with others. Write about this need.

5. Choose the image on your collage that shows the most important benefit you can receive from connections at this time.

6. Determine one thing you could do to improve or develop a connection with another person that does not decrease your independence and that can increase effective interdependence.

Relationships

MANAGING TRAUMATIC STRESS
THROUGH ART
© SIDRAN PRESS, 1995

26 | Worldview

Most people prefer to think of the world in which they live as a reasonably friendly and safe place. This allows them to be relatively optimistic about their current lives and future possibilities. Following trauma, people's beliefs and worldviews often become altered by negativity, hostility, and mistrust. Fear, disillusionment, and depression are other common psychological responses to traumatization. Traumatized people often yearn for life as it was before the trauma or for an imagined life that could have been had the trauma not occurred. Such longings reflect the need for a more positive worldview—one with increased comfort, support, pleasure, trust, and security. The first step in creating a healthier worldview is to refrain from denying your current situation and recognize trauma's effect on your current outlook.

People who have experienced trauma often alternate between worldviews that are either all good or all bad, or they compare an unrealistically positive memory of life before the trauma with an equally unrealistic negative view of the world after the trauma. Healing cannot be accomplished by resuming a previously held worldview, accepting a hopelessly negative worldview, or adopting an illusion that the world is danger-free. Construction of a more balanced worldview involves moving from a position of disillusionment and despair to one of cautious hope. In order to function at a comfortable level on a day-to-day basis, you must shift your worldview from one based primarily on the effects of trauma to a more realistic one that encompasses both negative and positive factors.

Part 1 of this art experience helps you to identify the effects of trauma on your worldview and to compare that to an idealized worldview. Part 2 helps you to transform your worldview. First you will be creating two collages to depict opposite worldviews: one that is affected by trauma and one that is free from this negative impact. Then in Part 2 you will be combining these collages to create a new worldview.

Estimated Completion Time 60 - 90 minutes

Art Materials

- one sheet of 18" × 24" white drawing paper or colored construction paper cut into two 12" × 18" pieces
- one sheet of 18" × 24" white drawing paper
- circular shapes in the APPENDIX
- acrylic paints (brushes, palette, and water)
- magazines
- scissors
- glue

PART 1: TWO DIFFERENT WORLDS

Getting Started

1. List several ways your worldview has been affected by traumatic experience.

2. List several features of your vision of an ideal world.

Worldview

MANAGING TRAUMATIC STRESS
THROUGH ART
© SIDRAN PRESS, 1995

Artmaking Guidelines

1. Remove the circular shapes from the APPENDIX.

2. Create the first artwork:

    a. Fill in one globe with lines, shapes, colors, and images, using paint and/or magazine pictures to depict how your worldview has been affected by traumatic experience.

    b. Cut out this globe and set it aside.

    c. Consider how this worldview makes you feel. Choose a color to represent this feeling.

    d. Create a 12" × 18" background featuring this color with colored construction paper or paint on white drawing paper.

    e. Place your completed globe on the background. Do *not* glue it to the surface. Set it aside.

3. Create a second artwork:

    a. Fill in the second globe with lines, shapes, colors, and images, using paint and/or magazine pictures to depict your ideal world.

    b. Cut out the globe and set it aside.

    c. Consider how this worldview would make you feel. Choose a color to represent this feeling.

    d. Create a 12" × 18" background featuring this color with either colored construction paper or paint on white drawing paper.

    e. Place this globe on the background. Do *not* glue it to the surface.

Worldview

MANAGING TRAUMATIC STRESS
THROUGH ART
© SIDRAN PRESS, 1995

Written Reflections

1. Place the two artworks next to each other. In what ways are they visibly similar and different?

2. Describe the feelings you experienced while making each artwork.

3. List the features you like about each artwork.

4. List the features you dislike about each artwork.

Worldview

MANAGING TRAUMATIC STRESS
THROUGH ART
© SIDRAN PRESS, 1995

PART 2: GLOBAL REVISION

Getting Started

Begin by looking at the two completed artworks from Part 1.

Artmaking Guidelines

1. Create one piece of art by rearranging and combining the two works you completed in Part 1. You may want to cut or tear the globes and backgrounds. You can choose to use all, or only parts, of the two works. Take time to experiment with different compositions to find one that is meaningful to you and representative of a transformed worldview.

2. Glue the elements together to complete this collage.

Worldview

Written Reflections

1. Describe what you find most striking about this artwork. Why?

2. Explain what role each of the world views created in Part 1 plays in this new composition. Does one viewpoint dominate the arrangement or are they represented equally? What is the significance of their relative importance to you?

3. Describe how the two different worldviews were modified during the process of combining them.

4. Consider how these modifications (noted in question 3) may apply to your healing process.

Worldview

MANAGING TRAUMATIC STRESS
THROUGH ART
© SIDRAN PRESS, 1995

Appendix

Appendix

Describing Your Feelings

HAPPY

adequate	contented	glad	proud
amused	delighted	glorious	satisfied
at ease	ecstatic	grateful	secure
blissful	elated	inspired	serene
calm	encouraged	joyful	successful
cheerful	enthusiastic	jubilant	terrific
comfortable	excited	lovely	thrilled
comical	fine	overjoyed	triumphant
congenial	free	pleasant	vivacious

SAD

abandoned	desparate	hopeless	pathetic
alienated	desolate	horrible	pitiful
alone	dismal	humiliated	regretful
awful	empty	hurt	rejected
battered	excluded	let-down	rotten
blue	forlorn	lonely	ruined
crushed	forsaken	lousy	tearful
defeated	gloomy	low	terrible
degraded	glum	miserable	unhappy
depressed	grief stricken	mistreated	unloved
disappointed	hated	moody	unworthy
discouraged	helpless	mournful	worthless

WEAK

cowardly	fragile	inept	unable
defective	frail	insecure	uncertain
demoralized	helpless	maimed	unqualified
disabled	impotent	powerless	useless
exhausted	inadequate	shaken	vulnerable
exposed	incompetent	sickly	weak

STRONG

able	courageous	fearless	motivated
adequate	daring	forceful	powerful
adventurous	determined	hardy	robust
bold	dynamic	healthy	secure
brave	eager	heroic	spirited
capable	effective	important	stable
confident	enchanted	intense	sure
constructive	energetic	mighty	tough

NUMB

ambivalent	bored	indifferent	paralyzed

MANAGING TRAUMATIC STRESS
THROUGH ART
© SIDRAN PRESS, 1995

COMPASSIONATE

admired
adorable
affectionate
amiable
cared for
caring
charitable
comforting
considerate
cooperative
cordial

courteous
dedicated
desirable
devoted
empathic
faithful
genuine
giving
honest
honorable
humane

interested
kind
lovable
loving
nice
neighborly
obliging
optimistic
patient
peaceful
polite

receptive
reliable
sensitive
sweet
sympathetic
tender
thoughtful
trustworthy
understanding
warm

SHAMED

abused
belittled
defamed
defeated
disgraced

embarrassed
foolish
humiliated
ignored
inferior

insulted
invalidated
minimized
mocked
neglected

overlooked
ridiculed
scorned

DISTRESSED

afraid
agitated
alarmed
anguished
anxious
awkward
confused
dazed
defensive
desperate
disconnected

distracted
disturbed
edgy
embarrassed
exasperated
fearful
flighty
frightened
frustrated
helpless
hesitant

hindered
horrified
ill at ease
impaired
impatient
irrational
jealous
nervous
overwhelmed
panicked
reluctant

restless
scared
shaky
shy
strained
tense
terrified
uncomfortable
uneasy
worried

ANGRY

aggravated
aggressive
agitated
angry
annoyed
arrogant
belligerent
bitter
blunt
callous
cantankerous
combative
contemptable

critical
cruel
defiant
destructive
disagreeable
enraged
envious
fierce
furious
harsh
hateful
hostile
impatient

inconsiderate
inhuman
irritated
mad
malicious
mean
nasty
opposed
outraged
prejudiced
pushy
rageful
rebellious

reckless
revengeful
rude
savage
spiteful
stormy
unfriendly
unruly
vicious
vindictive
violent

Appendix

MANAGING TRAUMATIC STRESS
THROUGH ART
© SIDRAN PRESS, 1995

Describing Your Strengths

ability to work hard
appreciation
asking for help when needed
calmness
celebrating good things
closeness
collaboration
commitment
competence
conscientiousness
courage
creativity
curiosity
decision-making ability
efficiency
emotional responsiveness
empowerment
ethical behavior
faith
flexibility
friendship
handling of separations
honesty
hopefulness
independence
inner-directedness
integrity
intelligence
interest
intuition
knowledge

learning ability
logical thinking
love
meaning and purpose in life
moral purpose
open-mindedness
optimism
organizational skills
physical fitness
physical health
playfulness
problem solving ability
relaxation
respect
self-acceptance
self-awareness
self-confidence
self-nurturing
self-regulation
self-responsibility
self-worth
sense of humor
sensitivity
spirituality
spontaneity
strong will
thoughtfulness
tolerance
values
wisdom
work for delayed satisfaction

ADD OTHER STRENGTHS HERE

Appendix

MANAGING TRAUMATIC STRESS
THROUGH ART
© SIDRAN PRESS, 1995

Describing Your Art

Here are some of the words that can be used to think, write, and talk about the pictures you make. They are separated into two types of terminology—those that *objectively* describe what is observable on the page and those that *subjectively* convey the feeling quality of the expression.

LINE

<u>OBJECTIVE</u>   straight, curved, horizontal, vertical, diagonal, circular, angular, looping, stepped, undulating, wavy, jagged, spiralling, zig-zag, short, long, continuous, broken, thin, thick, light, heavy, upward, downward, faint, jumbled, sharp, random, winding, outlining, enclosing, smeary, radiating

<u>SUBJECTIVE</u>   dynamic, lyrical, calm, passive, blurry, delicate, drooping, wriggly, turbulent, solid, rigid, limp, flowing, spontaneous, wispy, uncertain, direct, scribbly, gentle, fragile, sensuous, agitated, elegant, forceful, intense, aggressive, graceful, ordinary, chaotic, activated, free

SHAPE

<u>OBJECTIVE</u>   circular, rectangular, triangular, oval, square, conical, wedge-like, trapezoid, irregular, rounded, jagged, pointed, massive, large, small, tiny, interlocking, sharp, precise, foreshortened, concave, convex, symmetrical, asymmetrical, uneven, free-form, geometric, biomorphic, transparent, see-through, dense

<u>SUBJECTIVE</u>   distorted, delicate, mechanical, blobby, animated, organic, heavy, light, dynamic, uninspired, unusual, creative, ordinary, graceful, massive

TEXTURE

<u>OBJECTIVE</u>   smooth, rough, soft, hard, rugged, sticky, grainy, silky, slick, fuzzy, scratchy, pebbled, prickly, nubby, ridged, pocked, uneven, coarse, stiff, woven, wet, dry, cottony, cushiony, feathery, fluffy, furry, spongy, fleecy, slick, firm, dense, rocky

<u>SUBJECTIVE</u>   sensuous, pleasant, unpleasant, soothing, disturbing,

COLOR

<u>OBJECTIVE</u>   dark, light, dull, bright, grayed, warm, cool, hot, cold, faded, matte, shiny, gradated, translucent, transparent, clear, opaque, glossy, flat, neon, metallic

<u>SUBJECTIVE</u>   shadowy, muddy, powerful, rich, quiet, serene, shocking, calming, exciting, invigorating, harmonious, dynamic, luminous, harsh, soft, dramatic, expressive, surreal, mysterious, underplayed, clean, dirty, wild, weak

COMPOSITION

<u>OBJECTIVE</u>   repetitive, rhythmic, geometric, formal, simple, intricate, empty, blank, symmetrical, asymmetrical, fragmented, complex, organized, filled

<u>SUBJECTIVE</u>   dynamic, mechanical, disturbing, stark, appealing, disorienting, monotonous, chaotic, tense, boring, moving, awkward, confusing, flowing, unified, fragmented

Appendix

MANAGING TRAUMATIC STRESS
THROUGH ART
© SIDRAN PRESS, 1995

Questioning Your Art

Now that you've spent some time with this workbook, here is a guide to learning more about the art you've created and that which you will create in the future.

The pictures you make cannot actually speak to you, but they can still tell you a lot. As an art therapist once said, "pictures are messages *from* ourselves *to* ourselves." What pictures talk about is partly the world (and your thoughts or feelings about it), but mostly about you. Your creative productions directly reflect your inner life in a way that can communicate information that might otherwise have no avenue for expression.

Although the process of making art can be anything from soothing to invigorating, the benefits of artmaking do not end with the product. As you might have noticed in your WRITTEN REFLECTIONS entries, what we create certainly *does* offer us feedback when we look at it carefully—and ask the right questions. The tasks in the WRITTEN REFLECTIONS of this workbook are models of a style of personal inquiry that can result in learning a lot about yourself. It's not that you don't already know it all (inside), but seeing shapes and colors on a piece of paper has a tendency to help you really focus.

Here are some questions you can ask your artwork to learn as much as possible:

- What is the first impression you give and what factors contribute to that first impression?
- Which of your lines, shapes, colors, textures, design elements, or images are most prominent? Smallest? Largest? Darkest? Fragile? Attractive? Distorted? Strongest? Central? Peripheral?
- How do your lines, shapes, colors, and textures contribute to your design?
- How do your aspects (described above) relate to me and my inner life?
- Which of those aspects are most relevant to me at this moment in my life?
- How do the relationships of different pictorial elements pertain to my own style of relating?
- What else can you tell me about myself of which I am not already aware?
- Do I have a typical artmaking style that is recognizable when I look at a lot of you? Does it say something about me in particular?
- What more can I learn if I continue to look at you?

One thing you should know about pictures is that, although they are honest, they tend to save bits of information until you are capable of recognizing them. For this reason, pictures can be revisited and questioned again and again, over a period of days, months, or years. Art is patient . . . it doesn't mind waiting until you are ready to learn more.

Art Supply Resources

Chaselle, Inc.
9645 Gerwig Lane
Columbia, Maryland 21046
1-800-242-7355

Daniel Smith
4130 First Avenue South
Seattle, Washington 98134-2302
1-800-426-6740

Nasco Arts and Crafts (Midwest)
901 Janesville Avenue
Fort Atkinson, Wisconsin 53538-0901
1-800-558-9595/414-563-2446

Nasco Arts and Crafts (West Coast)
1524 Princeton Avenue
Modesto, California 95352-3837
1-800-558-9595/209-529-6957

Pearl Arts and Crafts
308 Canal Street
New York, New York 10013
1-800-221-6845

S&S Arts and Crafts
P.O. Box 513
Colchester, Connecticut 06415-0513
1-800-243-9232

Sax Arts and Crafts
P.O. Box 51710
New Berlin, Wisconsin, 53151
1-800-558-6696

Triarco Arts and Crafts, Inc.
14650 28th Avenue, No.
Plymouth, Minnesota 55447
1-800-328-3360

Utrecht (West Coast)
3116 New Montgomery Street
San Francisco, California 94105
1-800-961-9612

Utrecht (East Coast)
33 35th Street
Brooklyn, New York 11232
1-800-223-9132

Appendix

About the Sidran Foundation

The Sidran Foundation is a publicly-supported, non-profit organization devoted to advocacy, education and research in support of people with psychiatric disabilities. The foundation is particularly interested in providing support and advocating empowerment for people who have survived psychological trauma, and has developed resources in this area. The Sidran Foundation Bookshelf is a mail-order book service providing annotated catalogs and home-delivery of books, audio and video tapes, and informational materials of particular interest to trauma survivors, their supportive family and friends, and their therapists. The Sidran Press is publisher of a number of books and informational brochures on psychological trauma topics, including the highly acclaimed *Multiple Personality Disorder From the Inside Out,* a collection of writings about living with MPD by 146 survivors and their significant others. In addition, Sidran has compiled an extensive database of trauma support and treatment resources and conducts educational workshops. For more information, contact The Sidran Foundation and Press, 2328 W. Joppa Road, Suite 15, Lutherville, MD, 21093; phone: (410) 825-8888 and fax: (410) 337-0747.

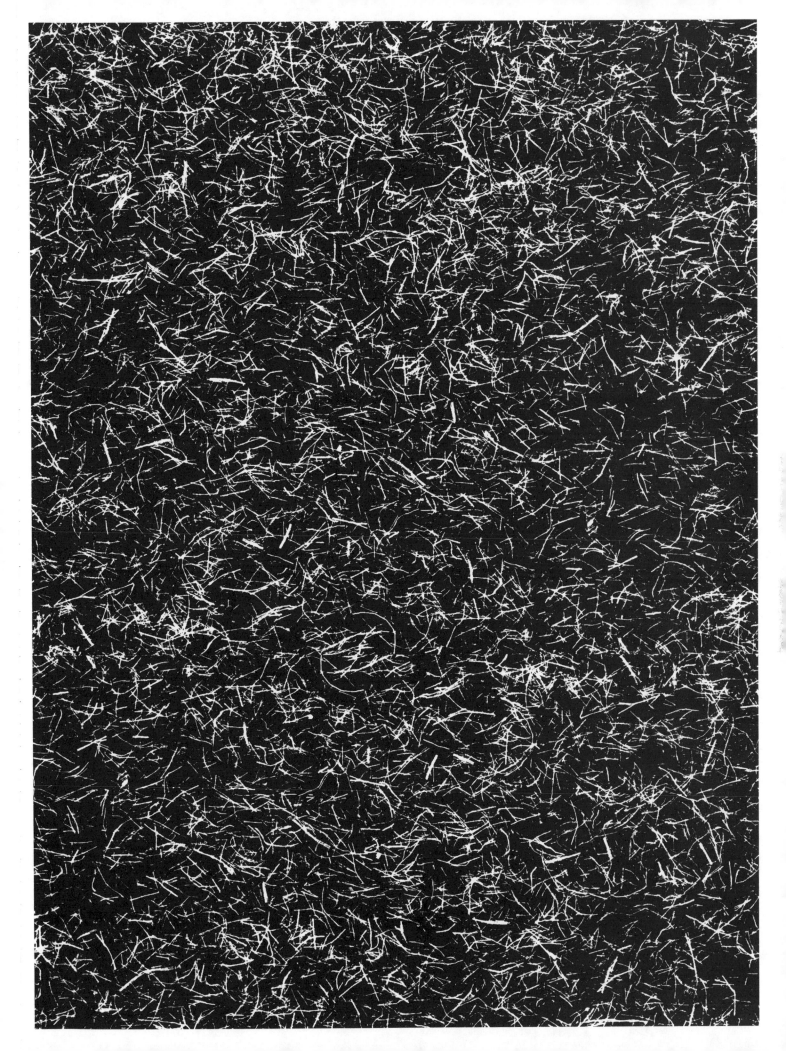

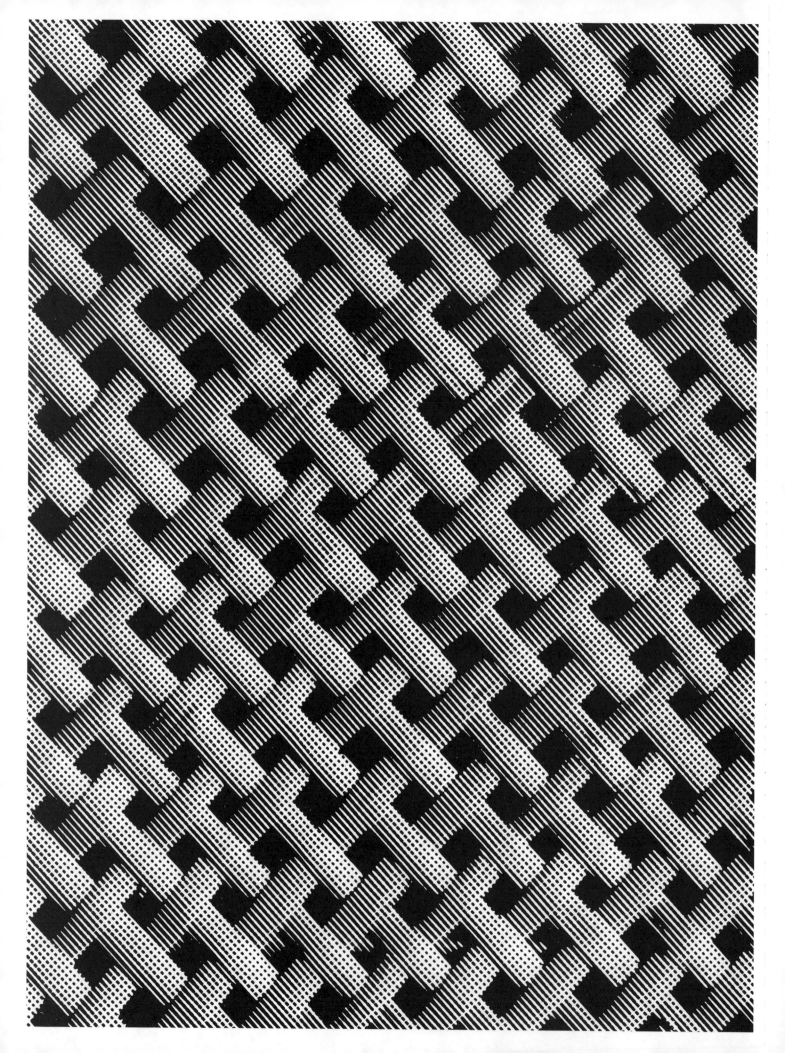

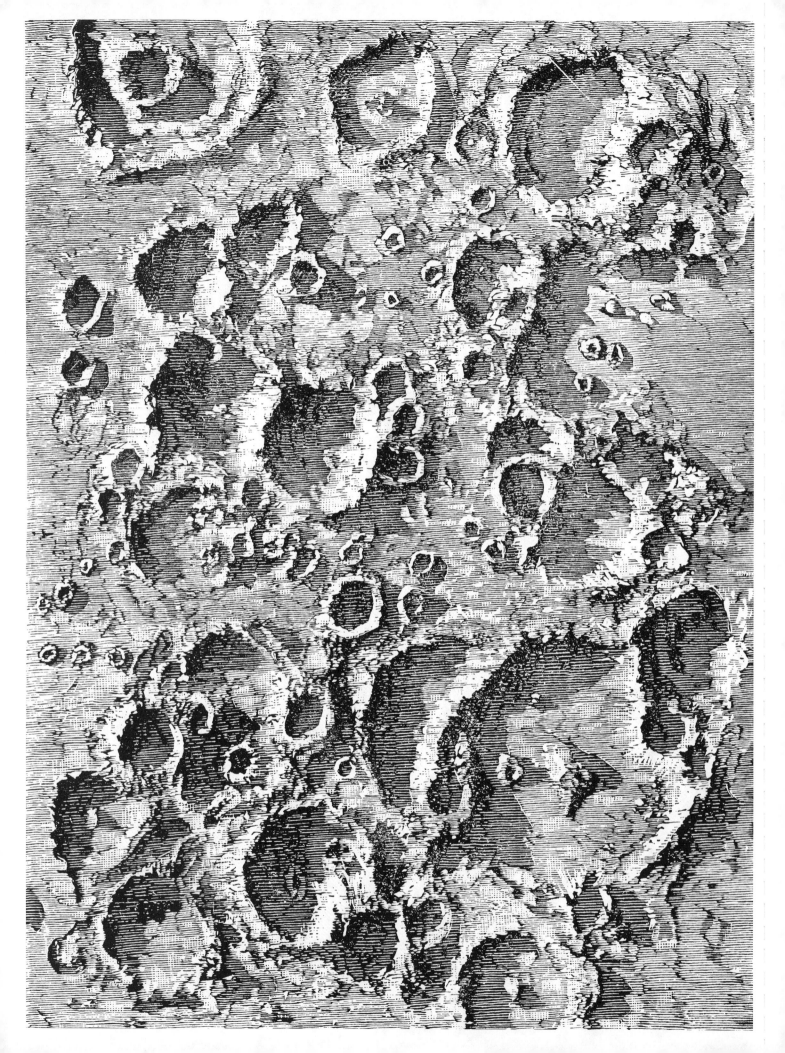

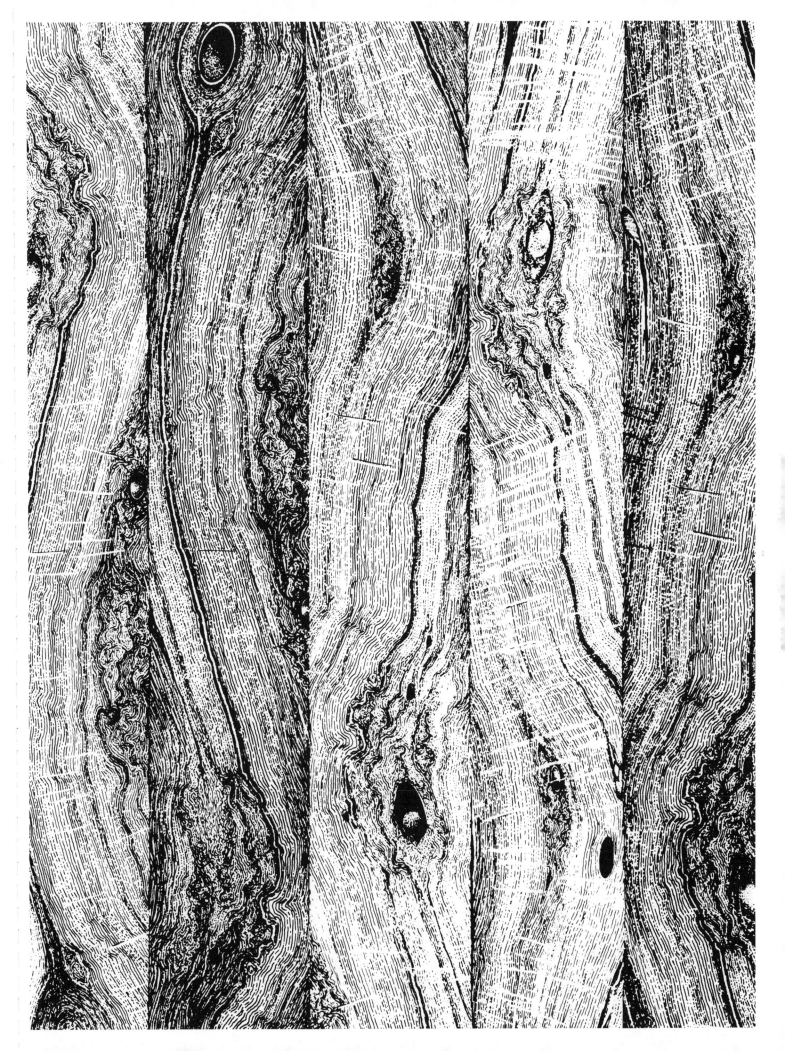

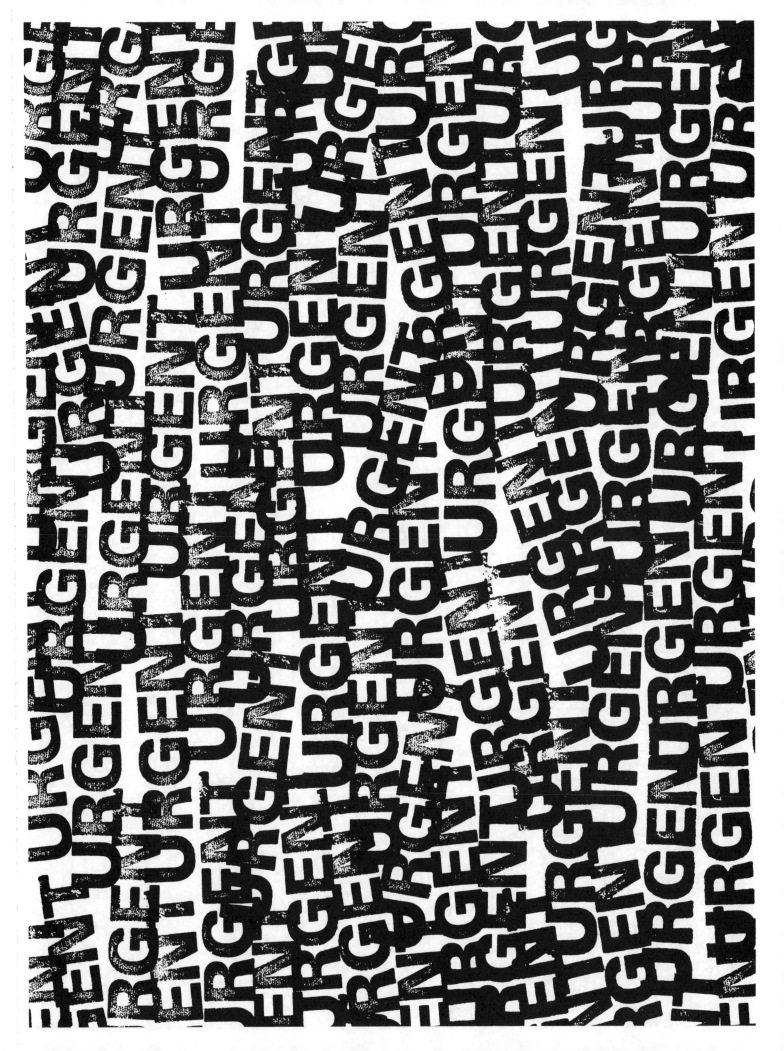

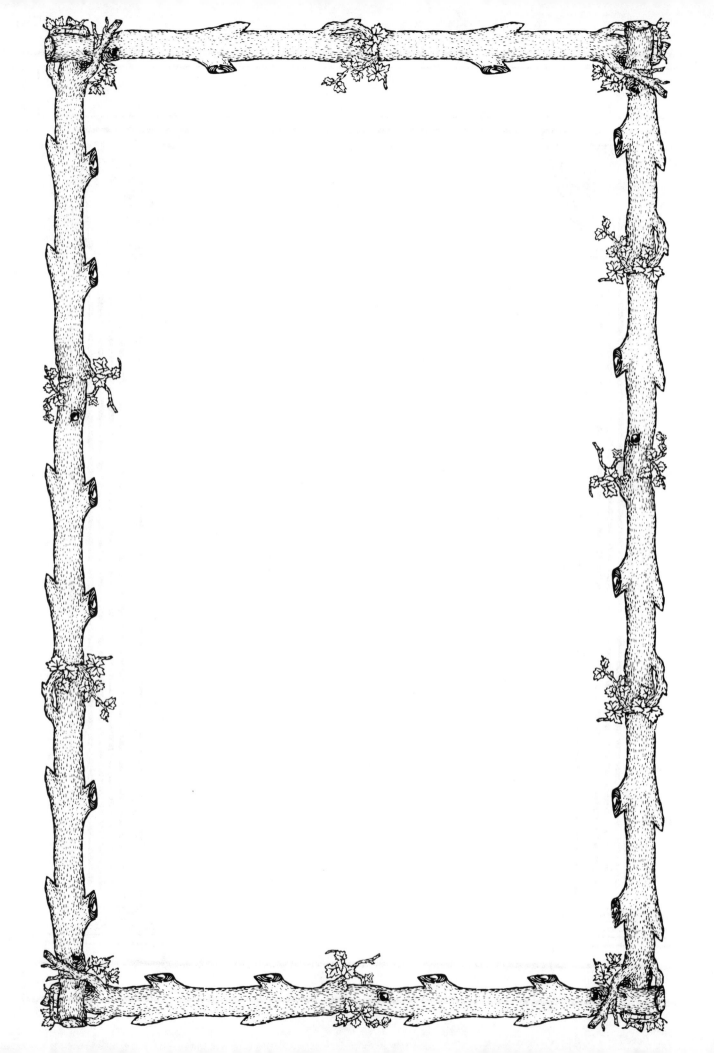

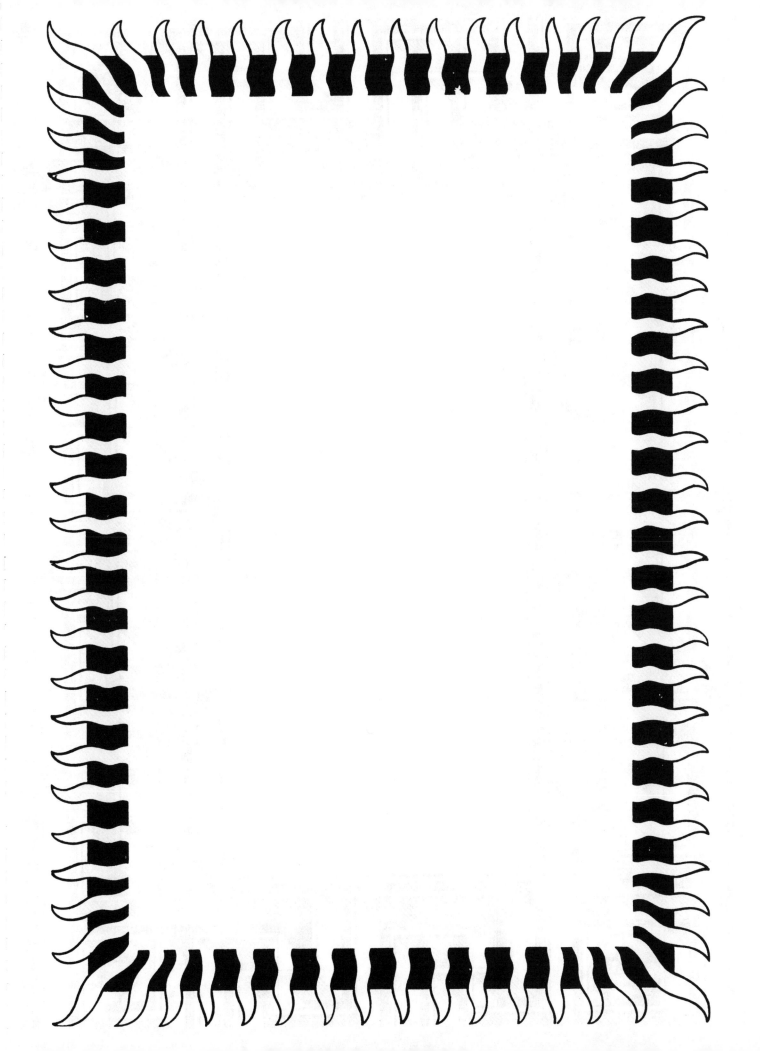

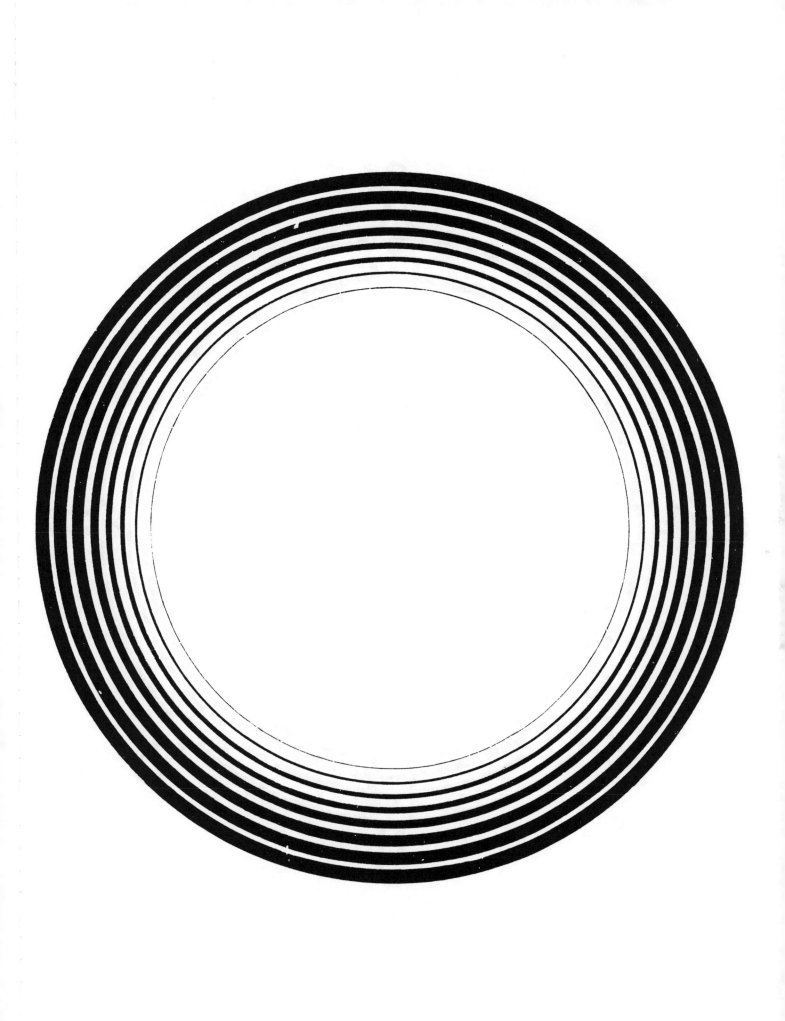

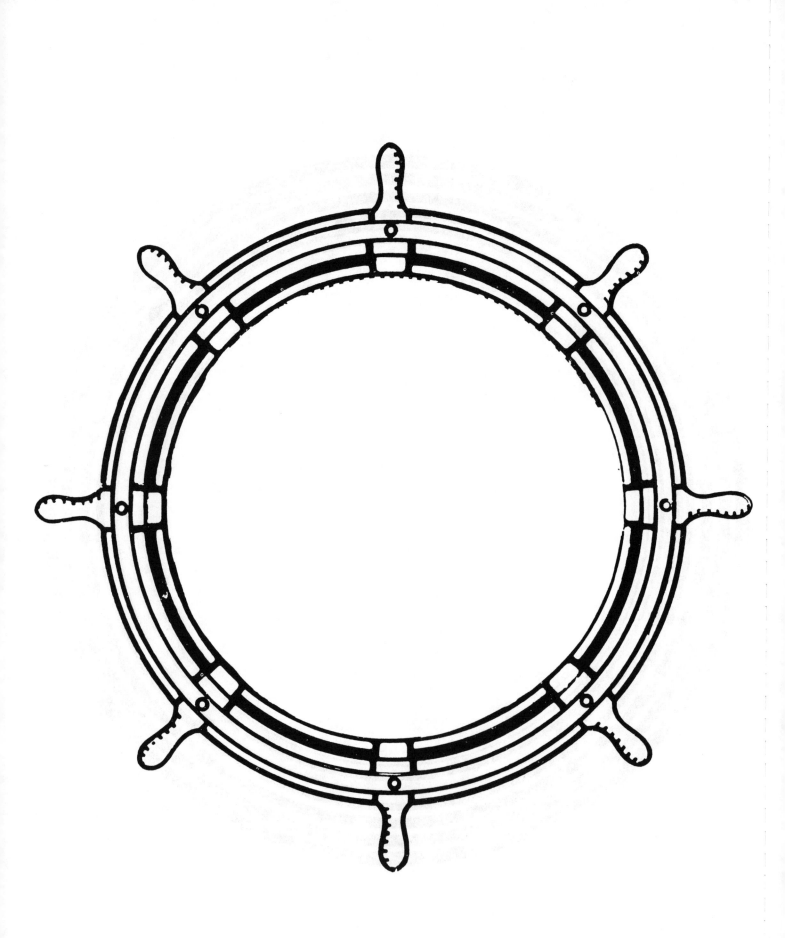

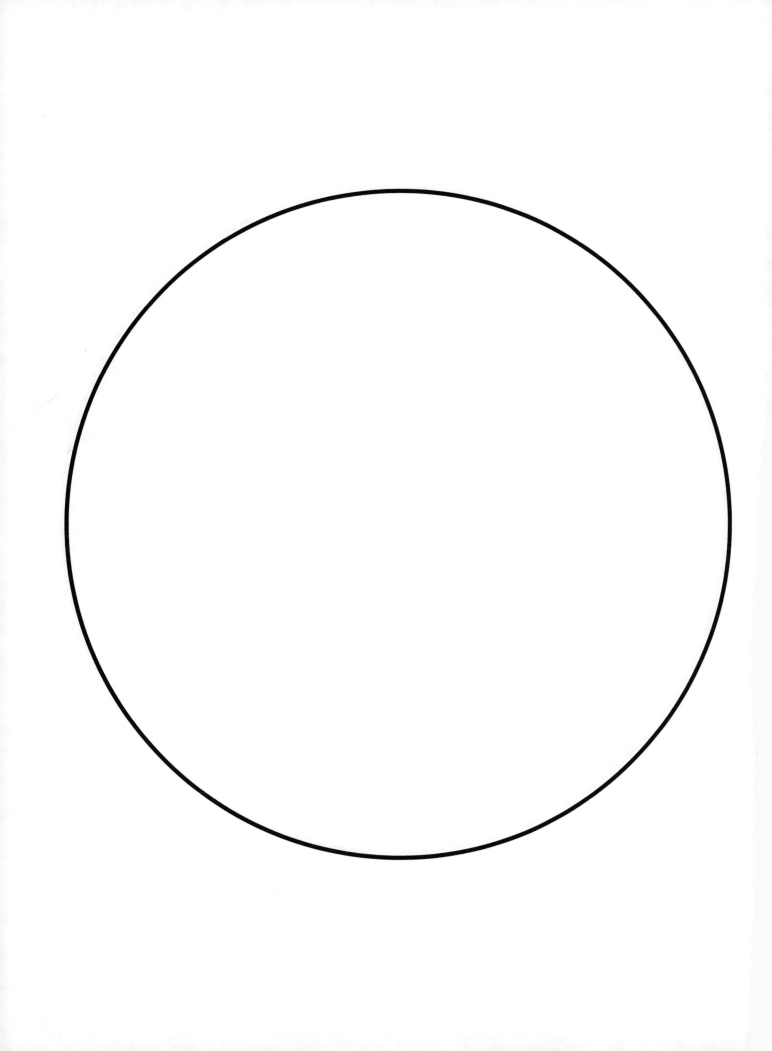

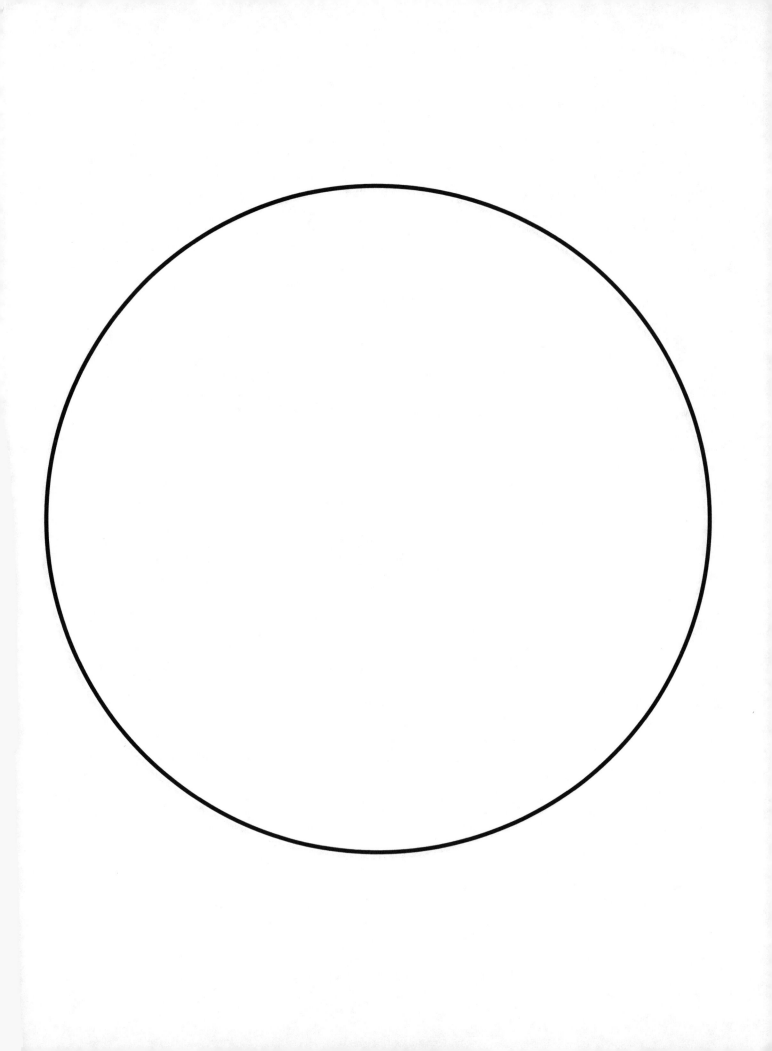

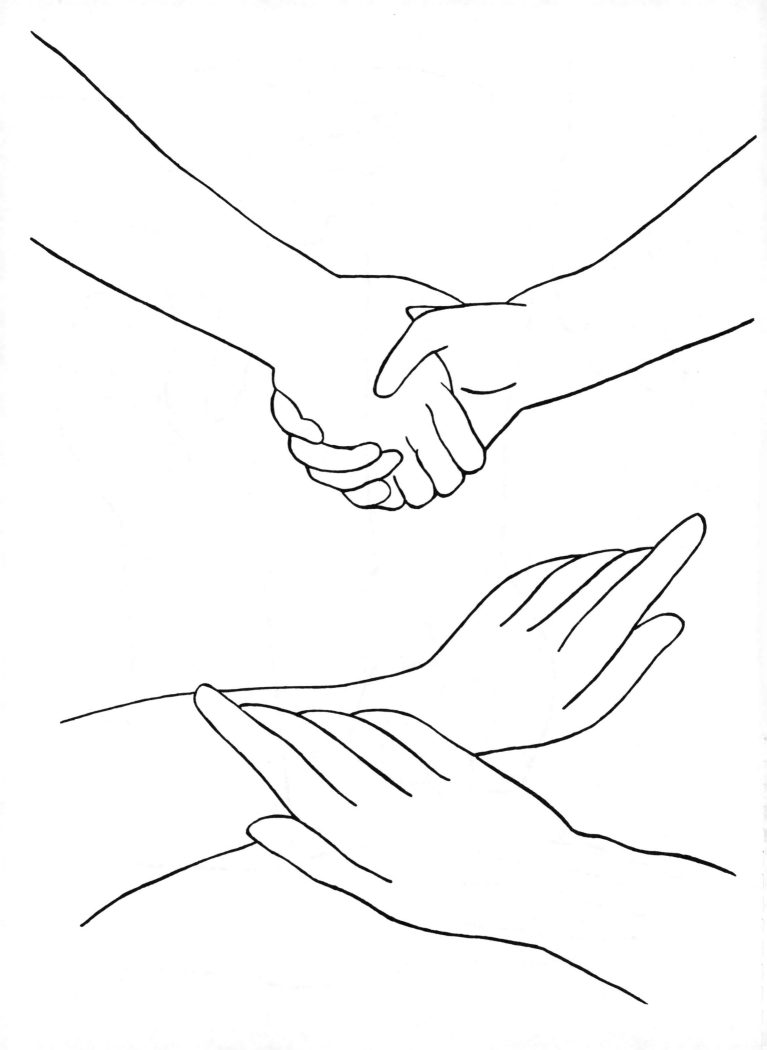

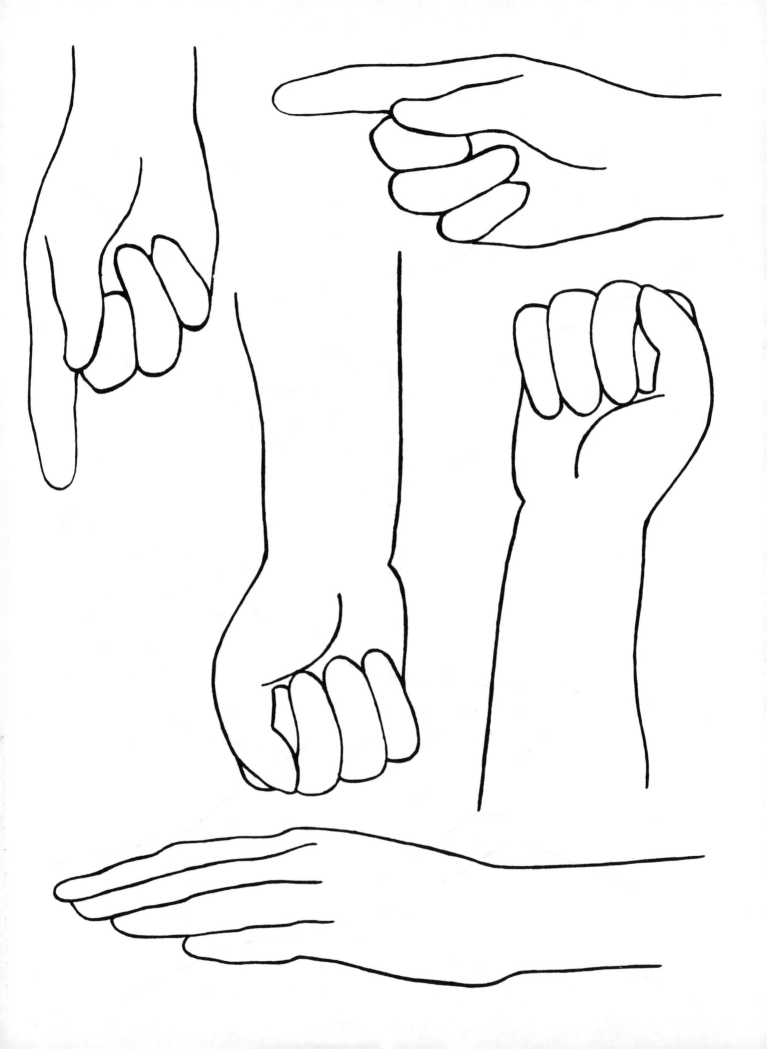

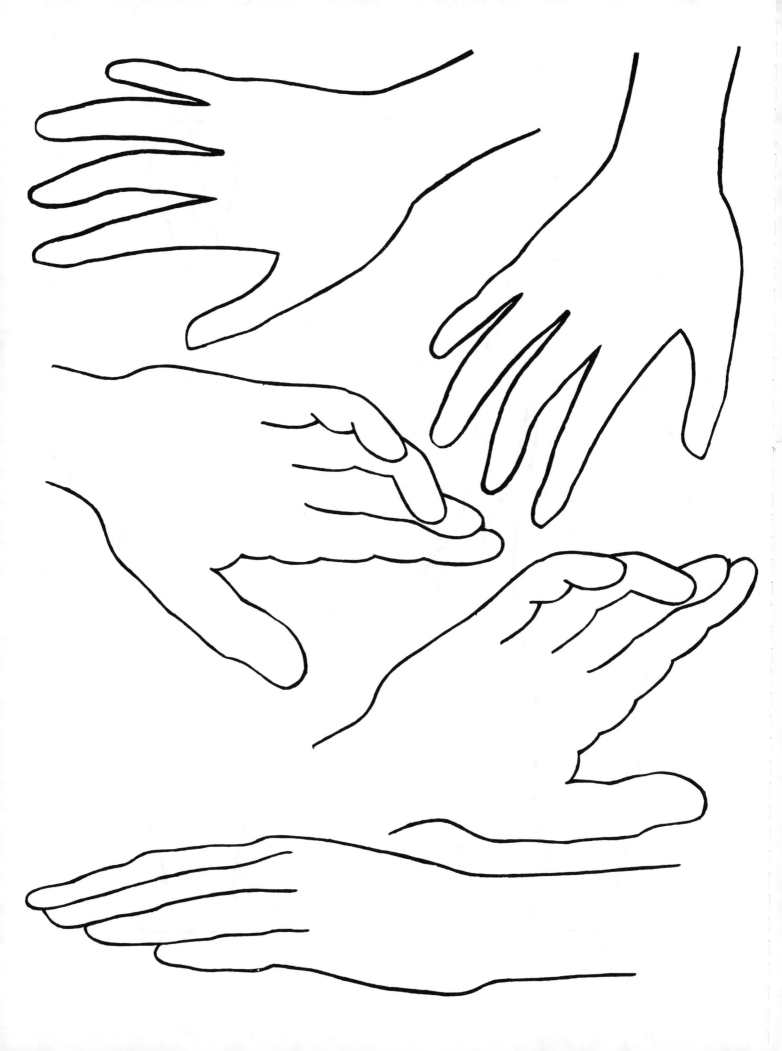

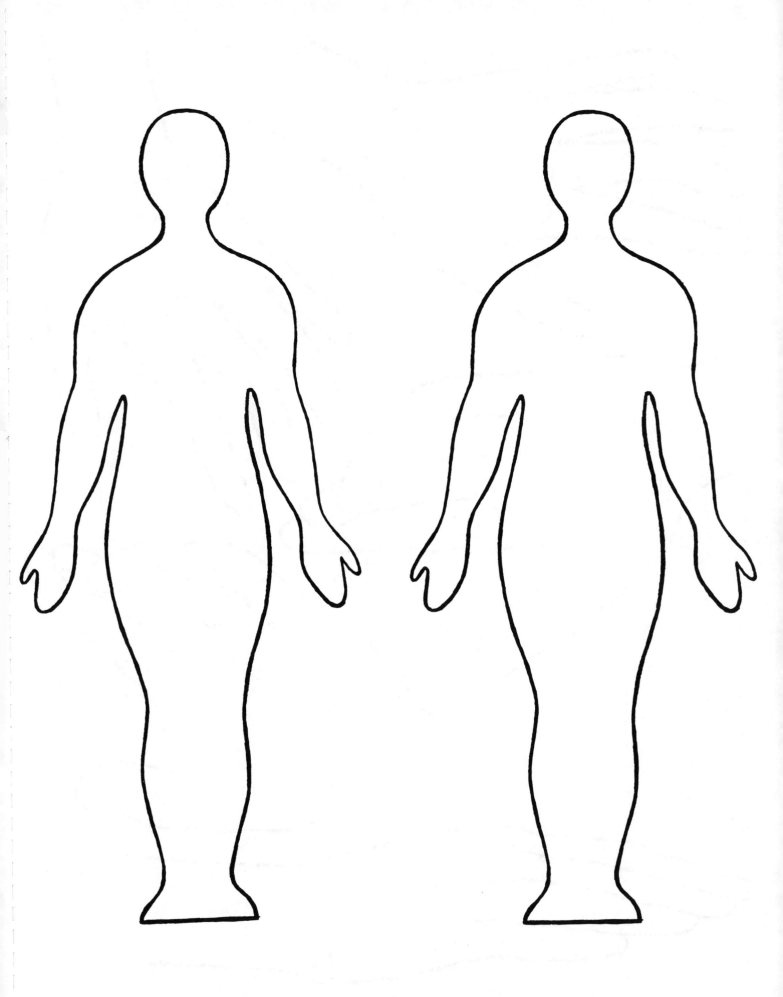

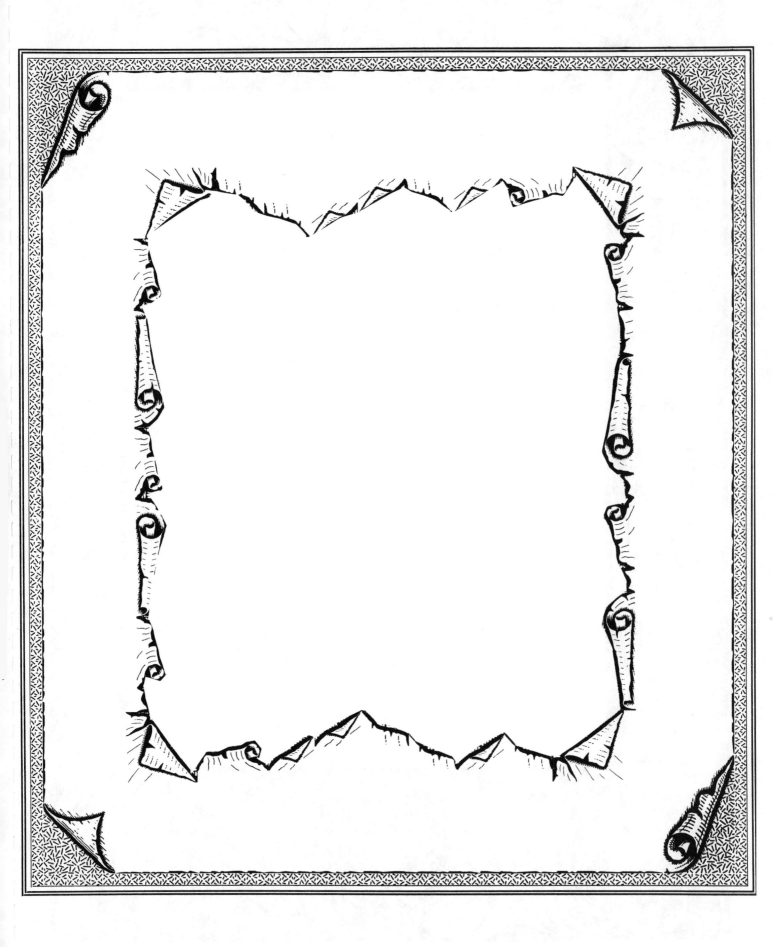